Even More Wandering Back-Roads West Virginia

with Carl E. Feather

Volume III of the
Wandering Back-Roads West Virginia
with Carl E. Feather series

Feather
Cottage
Media

Books & Images by Carl E. Feather

Even More Wandering Back-Roads West Virginia
By Carl E. Feather,
Author of *My Fathers' Land* and *Mountain People in a Flat Land*
Wandering Back-Roads West Virginia Series Volume III

Published by The Feather Cottage
6 Seaford Lane, Bruceton Mills WV 26525
thefeathercottage.com / carl@thefeathercottage.com
Copyright 2024 Carl E. Feather / Feather Cottage Media
Registration Number TX 9-390-448.
"Wandering Back-Roads West Virginia" is copyrighted by Carl Eugene Feather.

ISBN (paperback edition) 978-1-7330460-7-7
Library of Congress Control Number (LCCN): 2024905042

GOLDENSEAL magazine is a publication of the West Virginia Department of Arts, Culture & History, The Cultural Center, 1900 Kanawha Blvd. E., Charleston WV 25305-0300

Printed and bound in USA
First printing, March 2024

AI was not used to produce the contents of this book.

Front cover photo: Cook's Mill, Greenville, Monroe County (Chapter 7)

Other books by Carl E. Feather

Mountain People in a Flat Land:
Appalachian Migration to Northeast Ohio, 1940-1965
Ohio University Press

Covered Bridges of Ashtabula County, Ohio
Hidden History of Ashtabula County, Ohio
Arcadia

Ashtabula County: A Field Guide

Ashtabula Harbor, Ohio:
A History of the World's Greatest Iron Ore Receiving Port

Pleasure Grounds: 150 Years of Geneva-on-the-Lake,
Ohio's First Summer Resort

My Fathers' Land: Palatinate Immigration
to North-Central West Virginia

Wandering Back-Roads West Virginia (4 volumes)

Wandering Tucker County, West Virginia

Wandering Route 50, West Virginia

A Gathering of Feathers (Lenox Memorial Cemetery Feather burials)

Feather Cottage Media

Order Feather Cottage Media books online at
books.by/feather-cottage-media

Dedication

To Ken Sullivan, John Lilly, Stan Bumgardner,
and Laiken Blankenship

the editors of West Virginia's GOLDENSEAL magazine, who
supported my work and encouraged me to wander West Virginia's
back roads for decades.
God bless you.

Acknowledgments

Several of the stories in this book were originally published in the pages of GOLDENSEAL magazine, West Virginia Department of Arts, Culture and History. The author is grateful for their ongoing support of my work and the publication's focus on the people and stories of traditional life in West Virginia. Over the decades, I have had the privilege of working with some of the finest people and editors in the business: Ken Sullivan, John Lilly, Stan Bumgardner, and current GOLDENSEAL editor, Laiken Blankenship.

A big thank you goes to my wife, Ruth, for her patience and support of all my projects and books. Each day with you is a blessing from God.

I am likewise grateful for my father, Carl J. Feather, whose support of our work makes it happen year after year.

And thank you to all the people in this book, whose stories were patiently shared and images recorded during my back-roads wanderings. Your perseverance and kindness continue to amaze me; your friendships and the experiences I had with you will be treasured as long as I have breath.

Contents

Introduction

This book, the third volume in the *Wandering Back-Roads West Virginia* series, delves into a wide range of topics across the state, but you'll notice many of the chapters include the adjective "old." That's because nostalgia is the central theme in the stories selected for this collection. My use of "old" in describing my subjects is in no way derogatory; if anything, it is complimentary, for to reach "old" status one must survive many trials and threats. These are stories, therefore, about survivors and creators whose efforts persisted for decades and earned them a place in the West Virginia cultural landscape.

I am nearly 70 years old, and my heart aches with nostalgia for things of the past like my bones hurt after climbing a ridge. I cannot think of a better place to locate the liniment for those nostalgia aches than our Mountain State where change comes slowly and necessity preserves the ways and treasures of the past.

Ranking high on the nostalgia list of Baby Boomers is the experiences of seeing movies at the drive-in theater. In my childhood of the 1950s and 1960s, going to the drive-in was *the* big summer event. A drive-in was just a few miles from our home, and my parents generously treated me to that outdoor experience whenever a Disney, *Ma and Pa Kettle*, or other suitable fare was playing. I am sure those late nights in the backseat of my father's 1963 Ford Falcon contributed to my adulthood hobby of collecting and projecting 16mm films.

As I wandered the back roads and byways of West Virginia in search of stories, I photographed whatever remaining drive-ins and one-screen movie houses I came across. Two north-central screens were still operating, and I share their stories in this volume of mountainous nostalgia.

We also can be nostalgic about buildings, such as Mail Pouch barns, gristmills, barbershops, and outhouses, and I visit them in these pages.

Cherished memories of the animals that were part of our lives for an all-too-brief span also stir nostalgia. In three of our wanderings, you'll read about some special dogs that left paw prints all over their owners' hearts. Jessie Beard Powell's poignant story of her family's herding dog, Rocket, is especially moving for me because of his breed and silent-film fame.

Many of us attempt to slake our appetite for nostalgia by acquiring tangible items from our past, such as the furnishings and dishes we recall using at our grandparents' home. Roadside vendors, auctions, and junk stores help us make the connection, and they are part of this volume, as well.

In keeping with the practice of the prior two volumes, I also included a few profiles of the interesting people I've met on my travels: The former owner of Traveler's Repose, a poet/bookseller, the Mayor of Bowman Ridge, and artists who use their front yards as galleries for their work.

Thank you for coming along with me on these journeys. Many of them have been lonely excursions filled with uncertainty and disappointments (Chapter 15). More often than not, I "wondered as I wandered" if it was all worthwhile. I could have been at home settled in front of a movie screen watching Laurel and Hardy or spending time with my wife. Nevertheless I kept wandering, waving a documentarian's net across the countryside like a lepidopterist looking for a rare butterfly. I suspect I will continue to wander and wave until I leave this spinning cemetery and once again meet the many fine folks I encountered on the back roads of this great state.

As with the other books in this series, I reiterate this caveat: The *Wandering Back-Roads West Virginia* series is not intended to be a travel guide to the people, attractions, and places of West Virginia. The books are a documentation of the same—stories of the lives, passions, and trials of people who added a thread or two to the state's colorful quilt. As my late friend and fellow amateur historian Robert Harness said, "It's history," and, for that reason, I share these stories.

Chapter 1

The Old Repose

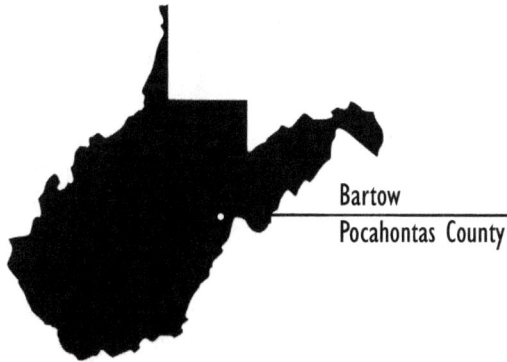

Bartow
Pocahontas County

Jessie Brown Beard Powell said many famous people spent a night or two at her family's Travelers' Repose in Pocahontas County. Unfortunately, she misplaced the guest register, so we must rely upon tradition. According to Jessie, that document would have shown that Abraham Lincoln, Stonewall Jackson, and Ambrose Bierce were among the notables who entered the arms of Morpheus within these walls.

Given its strategic location, age, and reputation for hospitality, there is no reason to doubt that these and many other famous people could have patronized the historic Repose.

The two-story, frame building stands at the foot of Burner Mountain and the intersection of Route 28 and the historic Staunton-Parkersburg Turnpike, Route 250. The young turnpike first birthed a hospitality stop in 1838. By 1845, the turnpike extended from Staunton to Weston, Virginia, and Andrew Yeager, son of Bartow pioneer John Yeager, offered here the first stagecoach stop west of Allegheny Mountain.

The mail route came this way in 1847, and Yeager's Travellers' Repose became a post office, as well. Its strategic location also brought destruction

Traveler's Repose stands at the intersection of Route 28 and Route 250, the Staunton-Parkersburg Turnpike. The lodge and farm are steeped in history and were caught in the middle of a Civil War skirmish in October 1861.

and death. On October 3, 1861, the area became caught in Civil War crossfire during the Battle of Greenbrier River.

During the prior month, the Confederate Army had established Camp Bartow near Traveler's Repose. That drew a Union response, and some 5,000 men under Union General Joseph Reynolds attacked the camp. Eight Union and six Confederate soldiers were killed; each side suffered 35 wounded. More than two dozen balls were hurled at Traveler's Repose during the skirmish, a Rebels victory.

Bushwhackers later that year burned the original Repose structure and thereby deprived both armies of its use. The Confederates, uncertain that they could hold Camp Bartow in another Union challenge, moved east about five miles and established the highly fortified Camp Allegheny to retain Confederate control of the turnpike.

The land they occupied was owned by the Yeager family, Jessie's ancestors. She says the intrusion of 1,200 Rebel soldiers onto her family's farm cost the family dearly; 500 of their sugar maples were cut down for military use.

Jessie Brown Beard Powell grew up in Traveler's Repose and returned to it after her travels around the globe with her husband, William W. Powell, who served in the U.S. Navy. She was photographed on the Repose's porch October 2011, age 96.

On December 13, 1861, the Rebels repulsed a Union advance on their new position, thus ensuring continued Confederate control of the turnpike. That advantage came at significant human cost. An unmarked grave on the property contains the remains of more than 80 Confederate soldiers who died of their wounds and disease that winter.

In 1869, Peter Dilly Yeager, who spent a portion of the war in a Union prison, rebuilt Travelers' Repose on the former establishment's foundation. The reincarnation had 22 rooms, plus space for 28 horses in the barn. Known as both the Yeager Hotel and Greenbrier Hotel, the enduring name has been Travellers' Repose, later Traveler's. Jessie Beard Powell told me her ancestors preferred the British spelling, *Travellers.*

Jessie's paternal grandmother was Eveline "Evie" Yeager Beard, daughter of John Yeager and sister of Peter Dilly Yeager. Evie married Josiah Osborne Beard; the couple had 13 children, including two sets of twins. One of their sons was Jessie's father, Brown Buren Beard (1883-1969), who purchased the Repose in 1912.

Traveler's Repose is located in a beautiful farming valley near the Virginia border. The road to the left ascends Allegheny Mountain, where the Confederates established their camp on the Yeager's ancestral land.

A perfect Repose

I visited Jessie in October 2011, when she was 96 and maintaining the Repose's tradition of graciously accepting passersby who stopped to read its historical marker. If Jessie felt up to receiving company, she welcomed these curious travelers into her comfortable home and shared stories about her favorite place in the world.

"I think the Yeagers named this place very well: 'Traveler's Repose.' I just love Traveler's Repose," Jessie said as she sat on a couch in the front room. "I guess it's because I've never owned anything else except this. My roots are here, and I've loved it from the beginning."

Jessie's beginning was May 6, 1915, when her mother, Nellie Blanch (Gum) Beard birthed her in a downstairs bedroom.

Jessie was the second child born to Brown Buren and Nellie Blanche Beard. An older sibling, Virginia Raine, died of meningitis at the age of nine months while her parents were living at Dunlevie (now Thornwood).

Her parents owned extensive land holdings in Bartow and Cass. Shortly after purchasing Traveler's Repose, her father removed the lodging section

Guest rooms in Traveler's Repose were simple, neat, and comfortable. Jessie kept a room or two ready in the event of friends or family visiting.

at the rear of the house and replaced it with four rooms for the family's use. Another addition came in 1928, resulting in its present-day configuration of a kitchen, sun room, dining room, parlor/living room, two full baths, two half-baths, and five bedrooms, two of which were reserved for Jessie's use.

A second house, to the east, was built in 1898 and was part of the estate that Jessie inherited. The neat farm buildings, painted white and trimmed in green, included a barn, granary, double corn crib, well house, woodshed, cellar house and storage building. Most of the farm buildings were erected by her father during the period that Travelers' Repose transitioned from hospitality to farming.

A progressive man of many talents and interests, Brown Buren Beard was Pocahontas County deputy assessor for the Green Bank Division from 1916 to 1920; county sheriff from 1920 to 1924; and county commissioner for more than two decades. His term as sheriff was during Prohibition, and Jessie shared memories of her father's exploits during this "wild time" in Pocahontas County.

"He found many stills hidden in these hills," Jessie said. "There was this one family over in Dunlevie that my father raided their still on Sunday night, but he found nothing at all. They figured they had outsmarted him and started up the still the next morning. They were going full force when my father came back. He just seemed to have a sense about those things."

Jessie recalled traveling with her father to Marlington and being present for the moonshiners' court appearances.

"When I got big enough, my mother didn't want me underfoot all day. She'd say, 'Go with your father.' She'd get me all dressed up, and I'd go to Marlington with him. He'd set me on the sheriff's table. You didn't move, you didn't say a word, I did whatever my father told me to do," Jessie said.

Brown Beard, who Jessie lovingly referred to as "Papa," was equally demanding of his daughter when it came to assisting around the farm. As the only surviving child, Jessie's responsibilities were myriad and included those typically assigned to male children. Jessie recalled stacking 300 hay shocks in a day. "I worked like a farmhand, even when I was a little girl," Jessie said. "Papa said he wouldn't trade me for anybody in the hayfield. I just mastered the skills that it took to be a farm girl."

A tenant family with five sons lived on the farm and worked for Brown. "They did a lot of work on the farm, but I worked alongside them in the hayfield, just like a man," Jessie recalled.

Jessie's father pastured their cattle and sheep on their Cass land during the summer months. That necessitated driving the livestock down the creek bed from Bartow. Livestock also was driven on the turnpike from Highland County, Virginia. Highland lacked rail service, and the livestock had to be driven into Pocahontas County to make the rail connection. Later, a man with a hauling service took care of transporting their cattle and sheep between farms and markets.

Her best memories of growing up at the Repose centered on her grand-mother, Eveline Yeager, who loved to spin stories of family and The Great Rebellion at the fireside.

"(Grandfather Josiah Beard) shot his toe off when he was hunting on Cheat Mountain," Jessie said. "He took it out of his shoe and walked back home. I don't know how he managed to do it, but he somehow made it back. When (his wife) found out what he had done, she made him go back to the mountain and get the toe. He had to bring it back home and bury it. He had to do that; she said that's the only way she'd let him go to bed.

"Grandma was a pistol, she was something else," Jessie added. "She could play a tune on her false teeth."

Jessie's paternal grandmother, Eveline Madora Yeager Beard, was recalled by Jessie as "a pistol" who loved to spin stories of the Civil War and Traveler's Repose around the hearth.

Jessie Beard Powell collection

A fiddler stayed at the Repose one night, and he and Eveline played dance tunes on their respective instruments, much to the delight of Jessie and other guests.

Growing up the daughter of a public official, Jessie was accustomed to a constant stream of constituents knocking on the Repose's door in search of advice and assistance. Her father patiently honored their interruptions although his days were full of farm and family responsibilities.

"Always I have thought of him as a man who lived in a house by the side of a road and truly a friend of man," Jessie wrote in memoir of her father.

Perhaps the most touching memory from Jessie's childhood is that of a farm dog that her parents were given after the death of their first child. The dog was named "Rocket." The border collie moved to the farm with them and soon proved his worth as a herding animal.

"He was a wonderful dog," said Jessie, who was about six years old when Rocket disappeared. She said the family had left Rocket behind at the farm when they went to visit relatives on a Sunday afternoon, and Rocket was gone when they returned home. Although they searched and inquired for weeks, no clues to his disappearance could be found.

"Someone had taken it," Jessie said. "We were heartbroken."

Months after Rocket disappeared, Brown took his daughter to Durbin

Passersby who saw the historical marker in front of Traveler's Repose often knocked on the door for a tour from owner Jessie Beard Powell. The sign makes note of the area being the land of *Tol'able David,* a reference to the silent motion picture that was filmed across the mountain in Virginia.

to see the silent motion picture *Tol'able David,* filmed in nearby Blue Grass, Highland County, Virginia. Brown and Jessie were stunned to see their black-and-white border collie in the film. She said further investigation revealed that someone had seen a local man, supposedly the Beards' friend, leading Rocket across Allegheny Mountain with a piece of wire for a collar and leash. He was thus suspected of having stolen Rocket for the film.

Watching the movie and seeing Rocket perform a variety of tricks, it is evident that Jessie's memories of Rocket as a "wonderful dog" are well founded. In that film, directed by Henry King, Rocket is killed by one of the Hatburn cousins who terrorize the community. One can only hope Rocket's lifeless body in his final scene was just one of his many tricks.

"I tell you, it broke a couple of hearts. Momma and Papa really loved that dog," said Jessie, who displayed in her dining room a framed reproduction of a movie poster showing Rocket.

A historical marker outside the Repose also refers to this being the land of *Tol'able David* and mentions authors who found inspiration in this bucolic, historic setting.

Novelist Joseph Hergesheimer wrote a story titled "Traveler's Repose" that was published in the April 8, 1922, *Saturday Evening Post*. Ambrose Bierce, who camped near the Repose as a Union soldier, returned later as a guest and makes reference to the place in "A Bivouac to the Dead" and other writings.

Jessie thus grew up at a crossroads of history, transportation, and culture. A famous author or scientist might dine with them one night, a cattle dealer or honeymooners the next. Although Brown primarily focused on his farming and political interests, there was no escaping the essence of the Repose as place of rest and refreshment alongside the turnpike. A knock on the front door late at night signaled the arrival of a prior guest who was seeking a repeat performance of their hospitality.

Jessie recalls a memorable Thanksgiving when her family was called upon to share their holiday bounty with guests. A heavy snowfall stranded a college professor and his assistant at the Sinks of Gandy, and they sought lodging and sustenance at the Repose. The Beards had no sooner taken in those guests than an airplane with five college male athletes on board made an emergency landing in a meadow near the farm. All were guests of the Beard family that Thanksgiving.

"We had a hard time, Momma and me, feeding nine people, plus ourselves for almost a week," said Jessie, who at the time was a college student on break. "Momma and I were a little bit upset because when they left, Papa (told the guests), 'You don't owe us a cent.'"

Maurice Brooks, the Upshur County naturalist, frequented the Repose. Jessie recalls Brooks showing up at their home on a Monday morning with expectations of a hearty breakfast: eggs, country ham, a variety of juices, and biscuits.

"Momma said, 'I wash clothes on Monday morning,' but he insisted and said they were *so hungry*," Jessie recalled. Her mother agreed to prepare the meal, but she charged the guests 50 cents apiece, rather than the usual 35 cents.

As for the cost of lodging, Jessie recalled it as "maybe $5 to $8" a night. "The rooms, the meals were very low priced," she said.

Jessie's living room was decorated with items she acquired in her travels through Japan and other foreign assignments while her husband was in the U.S. Navy.

From a Repose to Japan

Jessie was valedictorian of her 1932 graduating class at Green Bank High School and received a scholarship to West Virginia Wesleyan. Although she wanted to study at West Virginia University, Jessie agreed to do the first two years at Wesleyan. She ended up staying there all four years and earned her teaching degree from the school in 1936.

She found a teaching job at Marlington High School, where she met the man she would marry, William W. Powell. They were married at the Repose on September 6, 1941.

A native of Dry Fork, William was a high school teacher with military ambitions. After he and Jessie had been married a few months, he announced his plan to join the U.S. Navy. "I wasn't very keen about it, but I really enjoyed my Navy years," Jessie admitted.

William became a commander, and his assignments took them around the world, including two years in Okinawa, Japan. William and Jessie had three daughters: Susan Elizabeth Powell Leister, born in 1946; Jane

Beard Powell, born in 1949; and Jessica Anne Brown Powell Cheatham, born in 1952.

Jessie insisted that her family doctor in West Virginia, rather than a Navy doctor, deliver her babies. Every summer, Jessie returned to the farm with her young daughters so they could experience the kind of childhood she knew at her beloved Repose.

During my visit with Jessie, she fondly recalled the experiences that she and William shared as he served his country in far-away places. While living in Japan, Jessie climbed Mount Fuji, an experience she recalled in detail. Living abroad also introduced her to creative pursuits, including making dolls and flower arranging.

"We had a good life, an interesting life," she said.

After William ended his Navy career, the couple returned to Pocahontas County and took up residence at Travelers' Repose. William worked as procurement officer at the National Radio Astronomy Observatory and cared for the farm. The couple also became involved in the Cass General Store, with William serving as the corporation's president and Jessie handling day-to-day operations.

William died of a heart attack while assisting a cow that was giving birth. He was 58.

Jessie's beloved Papa died Easter Day, April 6, 1969. Her mother died March 27, 1978, at the age of 94. Their deaths left Jessie in charge of the Travelers' Repose and the family's land and timber holdings.

Jessie insisted that the Repose and farm buildings be maintained to the high standards that Brown Beard and the Yeagers set for this landmark decades earlier. Nearing the century mark, Jessie lived independently with assistance from a caretaker. She occasionally accommodated a friend or family member who had long-time ties to the Repose, and in October 2011, Jessie opened her home and farm to the 150th celebration of The Battle of the Greenbrier River.

As part of that event, members of the Loomis Battery of Michigan brought a cannon. But when it came time to fire it, the re-enactors discovered they did not have a round shot with them that matched the artillery piece's bore. Jessie referred them to a collection of vintage cannon balls collected from the property over the years. One of them was a perfect fit. For Jessie, it was an "awesome" full-circle moment.

Jessie's desire was for Traveler's Repose to stay in the family and be preserved as the farm and inn that she knew throughout her life. She pondered and fretted about that impractical scenario during my visit with her in October 2011.

"I have a friend who uses the word 'awesome' too much, but I think it was awesome to have the original cannon here," Jessie said.

In the days following the celebration, the leaves on the hard maple trees that surround Traveler's Repose took on stunning shades of red and orange, framing the landmark with befitting splendor. Jessie, standing on the porch of the Traveler's Repose that October afternoon, grumbled about the way the tree trimmers had pruned the maples. Frustrated with the state of the world and its permissive morality, Jessie still spoke of being blessed with this unique property and childhood of responsibility. And she issued a warning for those who would take charge of this family's treasure after her final night in its arms.

"I try to put the fear of God in them if anybody ever wants to sell the Traveler's Repose," Jessie said. "I can't imagine anybody else living in the wonderful Traveler's Repose."

Jessie Beard Powell died June 2, 2013. Her three daughters, who did not live in the area, decided to sell at an auction all the property and contents associated with Traveler's Repose. Darrell and Kandi Pingley of Sand

Jessie Beard Powell was a delight to interview and extremely knowledgeable about the history of the turnpike region. She enjoyed all of the Repose's many rooms, but especially liked the sun room on the side of the building. She posed there for this photograph at the close of our visit in October 2011.

Ridge, West Virginia, purchased the real estate that included the Repose proper, farm, Confederate fortifications, and cemetery. The auction was held over three days in late September 2014.

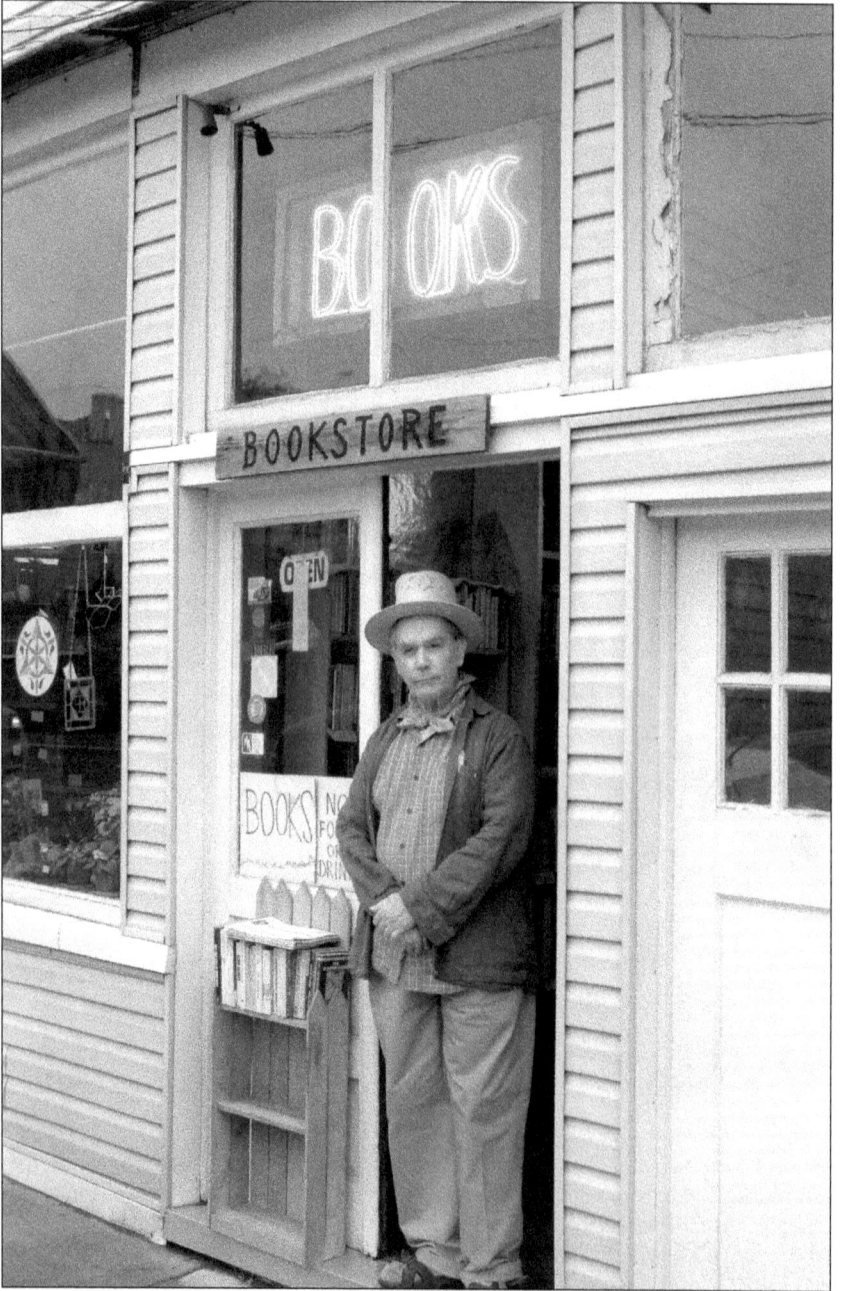

Poet and Bookstore owner Robert Head was watching the traffic slog through the rain in Lewisburg when I stopped and visited with him back in 2007.

Chapter 2

A Head for Poetry

Lewisburg
Greenbrier County

I spotted Robert G. Head standing in the doorway of his Bookstore as I passed through Lewisburg on a rainy afternoon in May 2007. Both the store and Robert, his neck wrapped in a red bandanna and head topped with a straw hat, piqued my curiosity. I turned around, parked, and left my wife to browse the shops of this charming town while I tracked down Bookstore's owner.

I found him deep inside the shop, where he was focused on the imminent arrival of Alfred Russell Wallace's *Island Life,* not the parade of "metal exoskeletons" (cars) on Route 219. Wallace's esoteric tome, due to arrive from the community college's library that afternoon, was an important link in Head's latest line of research: The Azores.

"I worked my way last year through Wheelock's Latin," Robert told me when I asked why he would want to research a distant island he's never visited. "I got so bored . . . The Azores are green, fertile. The Azores are very beautiful and warmed by the Gulf Stream."

Robert launched into an explanation of theories about tectonic plates and why one cannot sail directly to the Azores from Europe, even though they are in the North Atlantic. It has to do with the Gulf Stream, he explained. Someday, he'd like to visit the islands on a boat, not a jet. After all, Robert is the author of *Vultures Eat the Dead & Jets Eat the Living*.

The chapbook is among several poetry collections written and published by this bookseller/poet. Themes of injustice, particularly toward Native Americans, and man's self-destruction run through these thin but deep volumes of learned writing. "The Resurrection of Osceola" by Robert earned a first-place award in the poetry competition of the 2005 West Virginia Writers Inc., competition.

Ironically, he had turned to selling the words of other authors to make a living. "I make my living selling books," he said. "I break even on my publications."

Born January 7, 1942, in Tennessee, Robert had adored words since childhood.

"My father used to complain I was spending all his money on books," he said.

Robert studied the English language and its literature at a series of institutions, including Old English at University College, Dublin. He met there another American student, Darlene Fife. When he and Darlene learned that the United States was bombing Vietnam, they abandoned linguistic studies for a higher calling.

"We decided to return to New Orleans and exercise our rights as citizens to protest the war," he said.

Robert and Darlene edited NOLA Express, a radical, anti-war news-paper, from 1968 to 1974. Upon the suggestion of an acquaintance in New Orleans, they moved to Lewisburg in the spring of 1974 to care for a 115-acre wildlife refuge. Robert turned to selling books and opened Bookstore.

"I was tired of the big city strife," said Robert, whose activism had shifted to an anti-nuclear cause. "It seemed to me the natural thing. I didn't know how to do anything else."

Like the terse poetry he writes with all lowercase letters, ampersands, and minimalist phonetic spellings, Bob's storefront was tight and spartan, a chapbook squeezed by two fat reference volumes.

The storefront was defined by a set of heavy wood-and-glass doors, only one of which opened. And it tended to bind on the old wooden threshold and required an extra umph to open, just as Robert's poetry demanded

Robert Head was as interesting as the books he sold. A lifelong-learner, he was always pursuing his latest interest and research topic, aided by the inventory in his Lewisburg store.

extra brain cells to comprehend. Also like his poetry, there was more depth to his shop than its thin portal.

Bookcases made of thick, rough-sawed oak and other hardwoods lined a long hall that stretched from the front door to a slightly wider, brighter mid-section lined with more bookcases. Beyond that was an even wider room with more books and a platform large enough to accommodate the upright piano upon which Robert was learning to play Bach.

Above this piano was a self-portrait Robert from 1970. The long braids of hair he wore in that portrait had given way to shorter, graying hair hidden under the straw hat of an Amish farmer. He spoke softly, not as an angry, iconic anti-war protester of the Vietnam era, but a wise scribe at peace with the books he sold.

A young female customer came in and asked for Truman Capote's *In Cold Blood*. Robert steered her to a gentler tome. "I try to avoid books like *In Cold Blood* and *Helter Skelter,* gory, bloody books about murder," he said.

Robert said the atmosphere of Lewisburg, often ranked in the nation's top-ten small towns, was a good discovery for him and Darlene. Its amenities fit well his anti-automobile sentiment expressed in *Vultures Eat the Dead & Jets Eat the Living* .

"I don't own a car; I walk," he said. "I think automobiles are very destructive, and I think we are in Iraq because of the automobile."

Lewisburg gave him access to culture, the arts, and learning. He'd recently become interested in what he called the "soccer ball molecule," a complex manifestation of carbon. That interest inspired him to take chemistry courses at the local community college.

Language, however, remained his first love. He taught himself Coptic, Greek, and Latin to better comprehend the minds of great poets. "When you read (poetry in) another language, you read each word more carefully," he said. He also learned Portuguese.

"Mostly, I read Portuguese poets," Robert said. "They seem to be more serious than Americans."

Aside from having his poetry widely published and sold, Robert Head could find no avocation more fitting than Bookstore in Lewisburg. All the knowledge of the world was at his fingertips, except that one obvious question: How many books are in Bookstore?

"I let the books count themselves," he said, spoken like a true poet.

Robert Head's Bookstore was still in business the last time I traveled through Lewisburg, 2023. I looked for him in the doorway, but perhaps he was in the backroom reading an esoteric volume or playing a Bach invention on his upright piano.

Chapter 3

The Old Fiddler

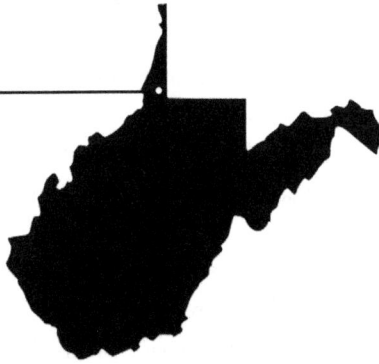

Bowman Ridge
Marshall County

As we settled into our chairs in his Bowman Ridge living room, Ivan Gorby tossed out a comment that caught me off guard and set a relaxed, jovial tone for our visit in April 2004: "A man told me the other day that he'd give $100 to see you."

"Really?" I naively inquired. "Who is he?"

"Some blind man," Ivan quipped, his eyes twinkling with the delight of a 90-year-old who'd just pulled a big bass from the old fishing hole.

Ivan was, by its citizens' proclamation, the Mayor of Bowman Ridge and had the paperwork to prove it. The ridge is one of myriad Allegheny Mountain foothills that rise abruptly east of the Ohio River in Marshall County. A casual traveler who ventures into this maze of ridges and hollows knows his location only by the signpost at the last intersection where he turned. I suppose you could enter this maze in spring and still be searching for an exit come fall unless you swallowed your pride and asked for directions to Route 2.

Ivan's house stood at the corner of Bowman Ridge Road and Rosby's Rock Hill, which descends the steep ridge to its namesake community

(Book 4). To the southeast is Sallys Backbone Ridge; to the west, Roberts Ridge; and to the east, Glen Easton and Goshorn Ridge.

There's no Gorby Ridge, however, a mystery given the family's ubiquitous presence in these parts since 1835, when Ivan's great great-grandfather John Gorby purchased 500 acres on this mountain. Of that original acreage, Ivan owned only six, sufficient for his garden, house, and apple trees.

More significant to our story, however, is the land that the Gorby family once owned but donated for the community's common welfare. The donation included the knoll upon which the Bowman Ridge United Methodist Church and Bethel Cemetery rise a couple of miles east of Ivan's home and, a half-mile to the west of his house, the land upon which three Gorby schoolhouses were built.

The first one was a log structure. Ivan said it stood on the south side of the road on a spot now a parking lot. The second was built 1894-95 and served the community until May 1923, when lightning struck it and it burned to the ground. The community rallied and built a third one. Ivan said it was constructed off-site in sections then shipped to Rosby's Rock on the Baltimore and Ohio Railroad. From there, it was hauled to the top of Bowman Ridge and assembled on the site of its predecessor's ashes.

Ivan attended seven grades at the Gorby schools, from 1920 to 1927. When busing became available in 1932, the board of education abandoned the building. The original Gorby grant provided that if the property were no longer used for education, the land and any structures on it would revert to Gorby heirs. The school board, however, saw things differently and scheduled an auction.

The day of the sale, Ivan's grandfather, Ezekiel Grant Gorby, showed up and challenged the proceedings. "Grandpa said, 'You can't sell it,'" Ivan said. "And they said, 'Yes, we can.' And Grandpa said, 'Let's go to the courthouse and read the deed off.'"

Ezekiel thus proved his point and halted the auction. Ivan said the school-board member declared that the building could rot for all he cared. "And Grandpa said, 'OK, let it rot!'" Ivan said.

The school did not rot; indeed, it was revived as a meeting hall for community groups like 4-H and the Farm Women (Bowman Ridge Extension Homemakers), which was organized June 24, 1937. With Grant's blessing, these groups leased the building from the school board for several decades.

Ivan Gorby stands outside his home on Bowman Ridge, April 2004. He was declared "the Mayor of Bowman Ridge" by citizens of the area, a show of appreciation to him and his ancestors for providing land for their community center.

Georgia Leach Jordan, who grew up on Bowman Ridge, joined Farm Women in 1947 after her husband came back from the service and they settled down on Bowman Ridge. Georgia's mother, Ethel, and daughters, Connie Crow and Shelley Jordan, were members, as well.

"We learned to do things, like make crafts, or we'd give to anybody who needed help," Georgia told me, summing up the organization's work. "We'd have socials there, too."

By the late 1980s, most of the Farm Women had moved away or graduated to one of the graves that dot the spines of these ridges like sandstone and granite goose bumps. They decided to surrender the building.

Bowman Ridge residents wanted to maintain a local place for voting, social gatherings, and playing music. They formed the Bowman Ridge Community Association and approached Ivan about using the building, which was technically still under the school board's control. "So, what I do is just lease it from the board of education for a dollar a year," said Ivan, who served as president of the association.

Membership in the association was $10 a year; a roster of paid-up

Originally built as a school, the Bowman Ridge Community Center served a small but vibrant community of residents who gathered at the center on Saturday nights for music and camaraderie.

members was displayed on a sheet of florescent orange poster board on the meeting-room wall. The roster, however, had not been updated since 2003, and Georgia guessed that total paid memberships amounted to only thirteen or fourteen13 or 14.

The community center was one large room with a wooden floor and light-blue walls. One section of the room had been the schoolhouse and retained the blackboards upon which Ivan and many other Bowman Ridge students learned to cipher and spell. The tattered roll-up maps, which were more historical oddities than useful learning tools, still hung atop some of the blackboards.

The original section of the community center also included a small kitchen and a unisex restroom that put the outhouse out of business. To make the building more accommodating to square dances, the association added a 16-by-38-foot section to the original schoolhouse, doubling the space available for community dinners, bingo games, dances, and jam sessions. Robert Harness, Gene Leach, Delbert Farnsworth, Shelly Jordan, Nick and Jean Frohnapel, and Bruce Diane Midcap did much of this work.

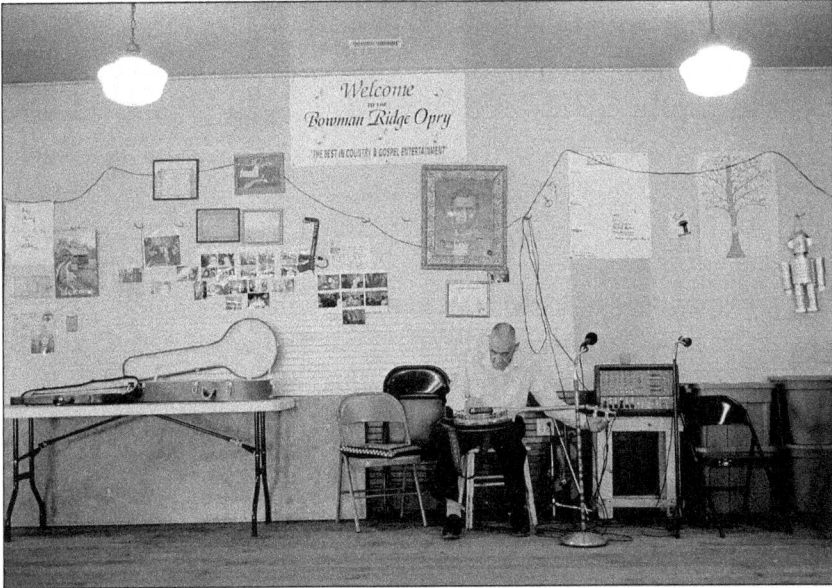

Ivan Gorby tunes his banjo as he prepares for a evening of music and camaraderie at the Bowman Ridge Community Center, Marshall County, in April 2004.

Decorating the walls were photographs of musicians who performed in the center, fair ribbons from the days of 4-H use, and a proclamation that shed light on how Ivan Gorby became mayor: "Important notice: After the votes have been counted and recounted, including the absentee ballots, by the Bowman Ridge Official Vote Counting Committee, the incumbent Mayor, Mr. Ivan Gorby will retain the office of Mayor the next term. Good luck Mayor Gorby. Truly a friend to all. 'Exceptence' [sic.] speech tonight 11/11/00."

An oak rocking chair, purchased by members of the association, was designated as the "Mayor's Chair" by a brass plaque on its headrest. It rested under a portrait of Abraham Lincoln.

Pointing to the portrait, Ivan told me that old Abe spoke to him when he stopped by the center earlier in the week.

"I said, 'What are you doing, Abe?'" Ivan said, setting me up for another joke. "You know what he said?"

"What?" I asked, knowing that, once again, I've been had.

"He said 'Nothing. Nothing at all,'" Ivan said.

Humor & music

Ivan credited Ezekiel Grant Gorby for this sense of humor that kept folks on their toes.

"Grandpa always liked to have fun," Ivan said. "I guess I was raised that way."

Ivan, the first of five children born to Perry and Pearl Martha Gorby, made his appearance on the ridge March 16, 1914.

"When I was born, my mother lacked just one of having twins," Ivan said.

Ivan's parents divorced when he was four or five years old. His father headed to Alabama. Ivan and a brother went to live with Grant and Amanda Gorby on their farm across the road from Ivan's birthplace. The three girls—Ada (Gonta), June (Barger), and Alice (Hummel)—went to live with their mother at her family's homestead.

His grandfather's farm covered about 130 acres. "We had cattle, sheep, horses, hogs, and we raised a lot of our grain," Ivan said. "In the morning before my brother and I went to school, we got up at five o'clock, cleaned the barn out, fed the stock, milked the cows, and separated the milk. Grandma would have breakfast ready, and we ate breakfast and walked to school."

Fortunately, the walk to school was less than a half-mile, thanks to the generosity of his ancestor. When the evening chores were done, Grant got out his fiddle and played it for the boys. Ivan says his grandfather never told him where he got the fiddle, but he knew it came into the family about the same time John Gorby purchased his land on the ridge.

"Grandpa's fiddle has been in the family 168 years," Ivan told me in 2004. "He was just a young kid when he got it. "

Grant sensed that Ivan had some latent musical talent, and when Ivan was either eight or nine years old, he asked him, 'Will you try to play a banjo if I go to town and get you one?'"

A few days later, Grant presented Ivan with a basic, inexpensive, five-string banjo.

"I had no idea how to play it," Ivan said. "Grandpa tuned her up, he showed me chords on it, and I got to playing with him."

Ivan doesn't recall the first tune his grandfather taught him, but he imagines it was a hymn. "He liked the church music, like 'The Old Rugged Cross,' stuff like that," Ivan said.

Ivan Gorby plays his violin at the Bowman Ridge Community Center, where Abraham Lincoln kept a watch on the activities.

Like his grandfather, Ivan played by ear.

"I listen to it and play it. That's all it takes," he said.

Once Ivan demonstrated his ability to play a banjo, his grandfather showed him how to play the fiddle and mandolin, as well.

"(Ivan) can play anything that has strings on it," Ivan's oldest son, Robert, told me.

"The way I think about music, if it's not born in you, there's not much use in trying to learn to play," Ivan said.

Several other musicians from neighboring ridges joined Ivan and Grant in playing music when he was growing up. They included Lawrence Games, a guitar player from Blake Ridge; Russell Emory, a banjo player; and Buna McClintock, an organ player, at whose house the musicians gathered for their jam sessions.

Tunes were learned from other musicians and by listening to the radio. His grandfather had the second radio set on the ridge. Grant and a friend who was manager of the Army airfield at Moundsville, spent six months building a battery-powered set and stringing antennas from Grant's farmhouse.

"They strung an aerial wire, I expect 200 feet long, about 30 feet in the air, and the first station they got on there was Omaha, Nebraska. Everybody was tickled about that. We'd have people over there every night listening to that radio," he recalled.

A social at the school, informal gathering at a neighbor's house, or church service provided venues for the ridge's musicians. A local musician rarely had the chance to play beyond the ridges or Moundsville. Many of the musicians attended Wheeling's WVA Jamboree, but rarely made it to the stage.

"This is the truth if I ever told it," Ivan said. "There was a feller out here on Lindsey Lane, about nine miles out, he drove a school bus; at that time you bought your own bus (and contracted with the board of education to provide student transportation). He'd come out to the forks of the road on a Saturday night, and if anybody wanted to go to the Jamboree, all he wanted was the 55 cents to get in, and we'd have a bus load to go in. Anybody who wanted to go to the Jamboree, he'd stop for you. All he wanted was enough money to pay his way to get in. Bonar was his name."

Ivan went to Gorby School through eighth grade. He said going to high school would have involved catching a train at Rosbys Rock and taking it to Cameron, the nearest high school.

"There weren't that many who went to high school here, there wasn't anywhere to go," he said.

Ivan Gorby makes music with Carl Ebert at the Bowman Ridge Community Center, April 2004.

He worked on his grandfather's farm until he was 15, then got a job with a housing contractor named Ed Masters. Masters built new homes along Route 250 during The Depression. When the Ohio River ravaged Wheeling Island in 1936, Ivan worked on the clean-up crews.

He was on a crew building a skating rink when his draft notice arrived in July 1941. His assignment at Randolph Air Force Base, Texas, was to Ivan's liking.

"I was always crazy about airplanes," said Ivan, who served on the Marshall County Airport Authority. "In 1927, Lindberg landed here at Moundsville, and it just seemed like I got attached to airplanes."

Playing cards against a backdrop of bluegrass music was one of the options for camaraderie and relaxation at the Bowman Ridge Community Center.

Ivan recalled being eight years old when he had his first ride in an aircraft, a German Fokker. As a result of his grandfather's friendship with the airfield's manager, Ivan spent a fair amount of time around the airfield. He recalled the day an Army pilot flying from Dayton, Ohio, to Washington, D.C., stopped at the airfield for fuel. When he was ready to leave, he asked the manager how to get to his destination.

"He says, 'All right, you take off and fly due east until you hit the Summit Hotel, and you'll hit Route 40 there. Follow 40 to the Chesapeake Bay, turn north and then into Washington, D.C.' That's the way they navigated back then," Ivan said.

Ivan's innate mechanical ability and interest in flying earned him stateside positions during World War II. In August 1942, he was shipped to the Army Air Forces Bombardier School in Big Springs, Texas. He received B-17 and B-24 crew-chief training, as well as co-pilot and aircraft maintenance instruction. He became an instructor, teaching cadets headed for

Bluegrass musicians (from left) Carl Ebert, Ray Cohen, Don Geary, and Frank Tharp jam together at the Bowman Ridge Community Center, formerly an elementary school, April 2004.

the war overseas. As a co-pilot, he was responsible for the aircraft once it was in the air.

While stationed in Texas, Ivan met his wife, Jayne Smith, an Austin native who was volunteering at a USO canteen. They were married September 19, 1942. After Ivan was discharged November 4, 1945, he and Jayne headed back to Bowman Ridge.

"I wanted to come back here," Ivan said. "That's what I wanted; to come back and build a house here."

Five children were born to the couple: Robert, Betty Ann (Estep), Linda (Delbert), Alice (Martin), and Jimmy.

Lumber was in short supply when Ivan returned to the ridge and purchased his plot of family land. He heard about a house in Glen Easton that needed to be moved, and Ivan purchased it for $100. He disassembled the structure and hauled the lumber to the ridge, where he and his grandfather built a modest dwelling.

"All we got out of that house were the floor beams, studding, and siding," he said. "It wasn't too bad of a house. They were wanting the ground where it stood, so I bought the house and tore it down."

Ivan wired the house for electricity, and in 1946 power finally came to Bowman Ridge. "We got a new electric stove, and the day we got it delivered, they turned the electric on," Ivan recalled.

To introduce the wonders of electric appliances to residents of the ridges and hollows, the power company set up a makeshift outdoor movie theater on the front lawn of Ivan's house and entertained the youngsters. Meanwhile, the utility introduced their parents to the wonder of labor-saving electric appliances..

Ivan was hired by Triangle Conduit in Moundsville in 1946 and worked there until retiring in 1965. He supplemented his income by repairing cars and other machinery in the shop he built in the basement of his house.

"He was Mr. Fix-It in the community," Robert Gorby said.

One of Ivan's traditions, growing horseradish for the community, came out of his car-repair business. Ivan said he did a brake job for a man who didn't have the $7 to pay him for the work. He paid the debt with an old-fashioned cider press, which Ivan used to make cider from the fruit raised on his property. He discovered that he could process horseradish roots in it, as well. In 2003 he raised, processed, and canned ninety-eight pints of horseradish that he grew.

Bowman Ridge Community Center

A few years before he died, Grant Gorby entrusted Ivan with the family violin. For more than 60 years, Ivan played the well-worn instrument throughout the Moundsville area at church socials, nursing homes, and community jams.

Every Saturday afternoon, Ivan packed up the violin and drove the half-mile to Bowman Ridge Community Association Center. With Georgia Jordan's help, he made the coffee and set the potluck table for the weekly "Bowman Ridge Opry," a jam session of bluegrass, country, and traditional artists. No one could recall when or how this tradition got its start, but photographs documented jams from the early 1990s..

"We've been here ever since we started it," Ivan said.

There was no cover charge for this gathering of friends, which got

Gene Leach and Pauline Beckett dance to the music of a bluegrass ensemble during a Saturday evening gathering at the Bowman Ridge Community Center in Marshall County, April 2004. Pauline and her husband, Ed, drove to the ridge from across the river in Ohio.

underway by 7 p.m. and continued until 11 p.m. every Saturday night, regardless of weather, crowd size, or lack of pickers. Sometimes there were just enough musicians to form a bluegrass quartet; other times, as many as two-dozen performers gathered to jam and learn from each other. Ivan joined them on the violin or banjo and usually performed a solo or two.

The association offered hot dogs and sloppy joes for a donation, and just about every person attending contributed a bag of snacks, a cake, pie, bowl of fruit, or plate of vegetables to the food table. After the meal, men formed foursomes to play cards while their wives doted on babies and shared family news. Those wanting a breath of fresh air gathered under a small picnic shelter alongside the road.

Ivan, the "ambassador" of the Bowman Ridge Community Association, welcomed each person who came through the door.

"These people treated us like we were family, like they've known us all our lives," recalled Dobro player Frank Tharp of his first visit to the community center in 1993. "It was just like homecoming. It's a good bunch of people. They enjoy what you do."

"It's about the fellowship mostly," said Don Greary, a bass player from Follansbee. "It's a nice place to come. We truly have fellowship."

Frank drove an hour to get to the venue, which didn't pay its performers. Like the other musicians, he did it for the camaraderie and smiles.

"If you can get them people sitting back there grinning like a butcher's dog, you know you are doing something right," he said.

An adviser with the nationally acclaimed Wheeling Park High School Bluegrass Band, Tharp described Ivan as "an old-fashioned fiddle, old-fashioned banjo player."

"He gets a little off key, but that's part of the fun," Tharp said. "The fun is getting back on key."

Some opry-goers, like Ed and Pauline Beckett, drove over from Ohio to enjoy the camaraderie and music. "Everybody has been treating us like we're family, ever since we came here," Ed said.

Even Howard Lee "Biggie" Byard, a Marshall County commissioner, occasionally stopped by to sing a few songs with the band.

"He's a fine gentleman," Howard Lee told me, summing up "Mayor" Ivan Gorby. He told me how Ivan had recently used an innocuous question as a springboard for one of his jokes.

"I asked him how he was doing, and he said, 'I'm getting so old, it took me two hours the other night to watch *Sixty Minutes*.'"

Ivan F. Gorby died April 3, 2013, at the age of 99. His wife, Jayne, died in 2009.

Chapter 4

Art from Old Stuff

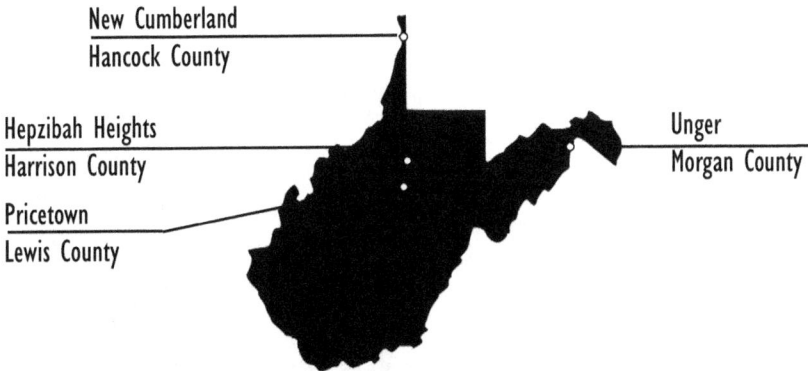

New Cumberland
Hancock County

Hepzibah Heights
Harrison County

Pricetown
Lewis County

Unger
Morgan County

I was wandering through Harrison and Marion counties on Route 19 when a red airplane twirling atop a 9-foot pole and a half-buried rocket caught my attention.

With a stagecoach, numerous deer figures, and a drive-theater movie screen also in this yard, I had a hunch that the person who lived on this steep hillside would make an interesting story. And that's how I came to meet George Harvey back in 2005.

George was friendly, chatty, and a bit quirky. A retired coal miner, his life centered on his faith, lawn ornaments, and a hobby hidden behind his garage door.

When I asked about the town's peculiar name, George said Hepzibah (that's pronounced HEP-zee-ball), was to the north of his property. George lives in Hepzibah *Heights*. Serviced by a one-lane road that is a straight shot up the steep hill, the heights consists of about a dozen houses and mobile homes. His neat, one-story, white house fronts Route 19 and is just a few doors down from the Hepzibah Baptist Church, where the town's name reportedly originated.

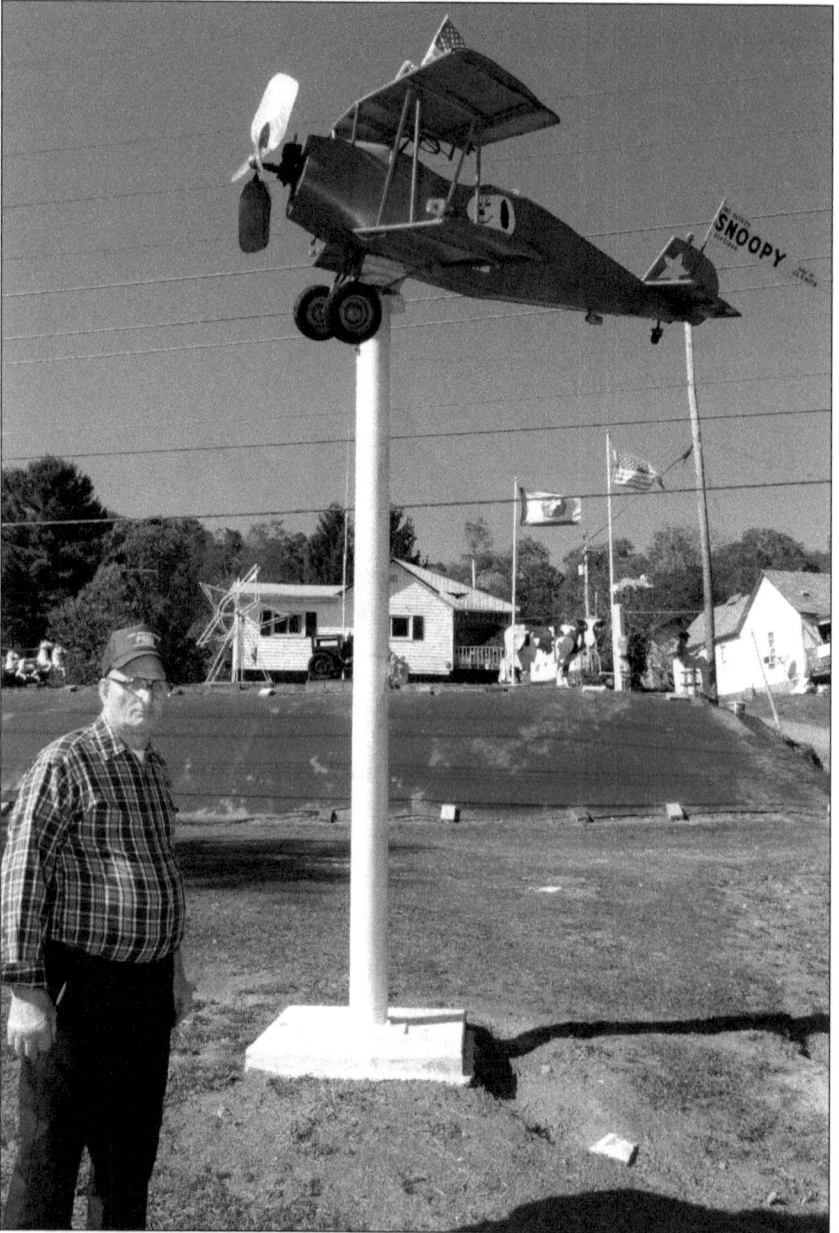

George Harvey of Hepzibah Heights, Harrison County, stands with the Snoopy airplane that his neighbor, J.E. Smith, built from sheet metal. After appearing in several parades, the aircraft was mounted to a pole as lawn art. In 2024 the airplane was still flying on the pole, although in need of paint, and George was still minding the property on Route 19 north of Clarksburg.

"This guy, he come through here and was preaching over to the church and it didn't have no name," George told me. "So, he said we'll call it 'Hepzibah.' He took the name out of the Bible."

The reference, incidentally, is to Hephzi-bah, the mother of Manasseh, a wicked king of Judah (II Kings 21:1).

Most of the decorations in George's yard were the work of his neighbor, J.E. Smith, who could build and mechanize just about any contraption. J.E built the red, single-prop, bi-plane of galvanized sheet metal on a frame of aluminum tubing. It has a wingspan of 10 feet, is a little over 8 feet long, and weighs more than 100 pounds.

The airplane reminded J.E. of the Snoopy/Red Baron saga from the "Peanuts" comic strip, so he painted a figure of the famous beagle on the aircraft. It was motorized with a 5-hp riding lawnmower engine and driven in several parades before it was assigned to the pole in George's yard July 4, 1988.

At Christmas, George put a little evergreen tree in the back of the plane and hooked up strings of lights to an electrical generator to the propeller. "The lights came on, but I didn't have any way of regulating it, so when the wind blew too fast, the bulbs would burn out," he told me as we toured the lawn decorations.

Brisk winds also messed with the plane's structural integrity. "The bolts come lose on the frame because there is so much wind up here, it vibrates them lose," he said. "I use a bucket on a front-end loader to maintain it with."

Other mechanized lawn ornaments, all the work of J.E. Smith, included a Ferris-wheel like structure decorated with Christmas lights and propelled by the wind; a 5-foot-long, 3-foot-wide locomotive built of metal; and a 6-foot-long stagecoach pulled by four plastic horses.

"They were his ideas, and I went along with him," George said of the decorations. He displayed them because, like the name of the town in which he lives, George likes being a little different.

"I wanted something different," he said. "Before the airplane was down here, I had a building in front of it, and there was a Volkswagen on top of it."

The building was part of part of another unusual attraction that George maintained in his yard. "I used it as a projection building," he said. It once housed two 35mm motion picture projectors aimed at a movie screen on

The "bomb" that landed unexploded in George Harvey's yard evidently missed all the deer and the stagecoach that were part of his lawn-art display.

George Harvey enjoyed projecting 35mm films in his indoor garage theater. The retired, multi-talented coal miner enjoyed "being different" when it came to his hobbies and lawn art.

the side of a second building. Speaker horns on the building completed the drive-in theater experience for his friends and neighbors.

"A couple of times they called the law on me and told me I was too loud," he said.

Some guys like to hunt and fish; George enjoyed projecting movies. It was his hobby. He would have continued to run the outdoor shows had the roof on the projection booth not collapsed. That forced him to relocate his projectors and associated audio equipment to his garage. At one end was an elevated projection room with two 35mm projectors, weighing a total of one ton, and a 16mm projector that was modified by J.E. Smith so it could use a carbon arc for its light source. At the other end was a screen 8 feet tall by 16 feet wide. J.E. Smith had secured the projectors and many of the films in his collection from a Fairmont theater that closed, and George took it from there.

Several huge speakers were mounted on the ceiling to provide a genuine movie-going experience, complete with an electronic keyboard wired into the sound system. George ran mostly westerns and Dead End Kids features, previews of coming attractions. He admitted that he was usually the only person in the audience. It was mostly about the joy of being a moving-picture operator and the freedom to be himself.

"I like to be different," he told me. "I am different."

I returned to Hepzibah and visited with George in the process of writing this book. He lives independently and takes care of his home and large yard, despite some mobility issues. His friend, J.E. Smith, passed away several years ago, and J.E.'s widow' has been in poor health. The airplane is still flying, although in need of some maintenance.

George's garage theater is intact and he still loves to project those old films. He said that it had been a few months since he ran any film through his projectors, and when he does, it is mostly to keep the system in operating condition. Several years ago, he relocated his enthusiasm for movies on a big screen to his living room, where a pull-down screen and digital projector satisfy his appetite for the projected image.

Also on his home's walls were several large-screen TVs, all of them displaying the feed from security cameras placed all around his property. With all those camera eyes keeping a watch over the grounds, George's lawn ornaments and theater are secure.

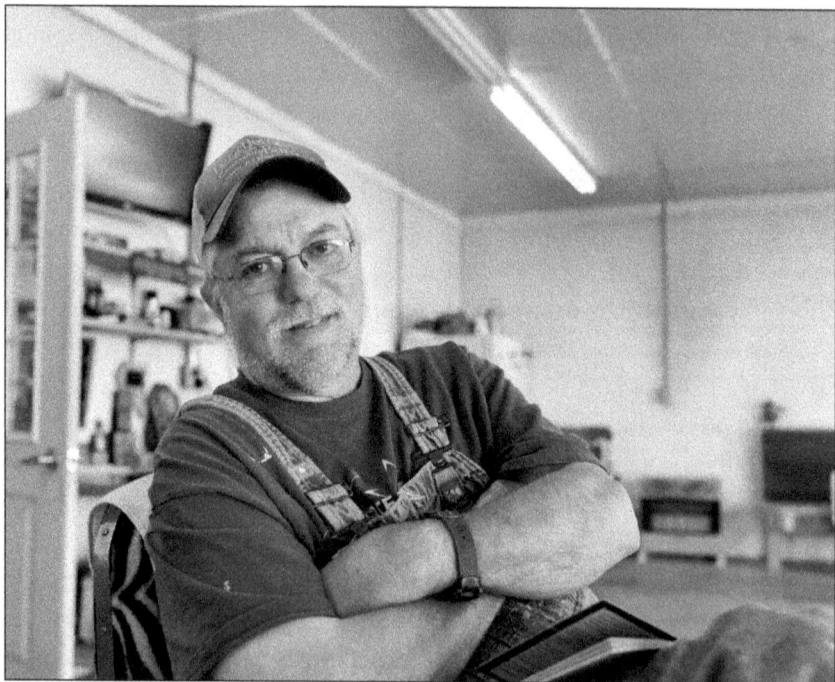

After a 35-year career as magistrate and owning/operating several businesses, Dan Moody was ready to settle down in a barber's chair in his man cave and make lawn art.

Magistrate turned artist

The same could be said for the lawn art in the front and side yards of James "Dan" Moody's place in Pricetown on routes 33/119. Dan was a Lewis County magistrate for 35 years and a law enforcement officer prior to that. He also owned a car wash, convenience store, and rental properties much of the time he was magistrate. When Dad retired in 2012, he was tired.

"Domestic cases are always sad. That's probably the hardest thing," Dan said. "And every night, it seems like you got called out. . . . My wife says I've been a nicer person since I lost that job."

Dan also closed many of his businesses as he transitioned to retirement; he said they would have killed him if he would have continued to run them. Leftover from those days of being a small businessman was a sign in his yard asking consumers to "Help the little guy," Being a "little guy"

Dan Moody's lawn art ranged from a lighthouse to spinning contraptions based upon discarded bicycle wheels. A friend provided the inspiration for the pole figure (left). His display is along route 33/119 in Pricetown.

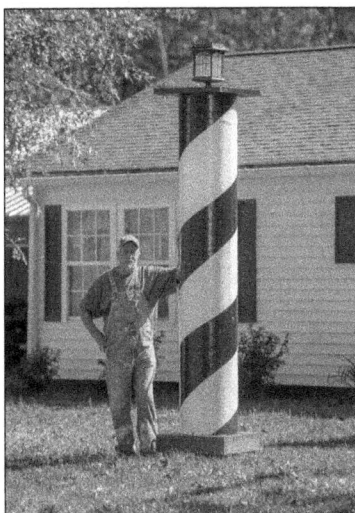

business owner myself, that admonition drew me to stop and talk about that and his lawn art.

I found Dan in his garage/man cave, where he was taking a break in his barber chair. Barbering was not one of Dan's many business ventures, but he fancied the chairs of the trade.

"I always wanted a barber chair," Dan said. "But people want $600 to $800 for these things. Finally, I found this one at a yard sale and I asked how much it was. The man said he'd take $150, and my heart started pumping..."

Dan has not been one to loiter in his barbershop chair since retirement. He still has business properties to maintain and enjoys making lawn ornaments that dazzle passersby. Like the late Jim Davis (second book in this series), Dan builds his creations from whatever scrap and discards he's found, along with some store-bought materials.

"I walked up and down the aisles of Lowe's looking," Dan said, explaining how he came up with the fins that catch the wind and make the bicycle wheels on his lawn art spin. "I found those plates that are used for building rafters. They are pliable and easy to drill."

The bicycle wheels, and a small bicycle, were affixed to a metal wheel 8 feet in diameter. That wheel was part of the core that once held fiber optic cable and provided this framework for his largest piece of lawn art.

Elsewhere in the yard, the collection included Snoopy flying in his red airplane, made from an old water heater and assorted other metal scrap, and a wooden character with horseshoes for his hands and a face that jogs Dan's memory of a childhood friend, John Posey.

A lighthouse that he built is a nod to Dan's passion for visiting the structures wherever he travels. "If I get within 100 miles of lighthouse, I have to go see it," he said. "I love lighthouses."

Dan said children looked forward to seeing the brightly painted wheels spinning in the wind whenever they passed by his home.

"I had a guy tell me that his kid starts looking for them three to four miles before they get here. They really enjoy it," Dan said.

It sure beats the magistrate's heart-breaking caseload of domestic complaints and criminal cases. It even beats relaxing in a barber's chair.

"I got to stay busy," Dan said. "I can't sit still. I don't know if that is the grace of God or a curse."

Ken Sinsel and his daughter Joy stand with a horse and alien they created from scrap metal. The life-size figures and other were on the lawn of their suburban home along Route 2, New Cumberland, Hancock County.

The iron horse

The most striking examples of lawn art I've come across in my wanderings were on Route 2 as it wends through New Cumberland in Hancock County. Ken Sinsel's front yard, which looks out upon the Ohio River, has become a tourist attraction thanks to the life-size creations he and his daughter, Joy, assembled from old scrap metal.

I visited with Ken and Joy in the fall of 2017. They explained how, in just four years, their front yard had been transformed into a gallery of lawn art. Each figure was artistically assembled from disparate scrap items that Ken welded into works of art.

His larger works include a life-size horse and 15-foot-tall dragon whose humps and tail appeared to undulate over the yard. Smaller pieces include fish, flowers, and whimsical characters. From the street, these pieces look like well-executed metal sculptures painstakingly assembled in an artist's studio using custom-cut materials. Upon close inspection, their real composition

Joy Sinsel poses with a fish that she created from scrap metal and junkyard finds.
Her father and mentor, Ken, is in the background.

comes into focus: thousands of bolts, springs, hinges, chains, car parts, and
tools donated to the artist or scrounged from scrap-metal yards.

Ken told me that as neighbors and passersby noticed his creations,
they began dropping off in his driveway boxes and buckets of scrap ferrous
materials cleared from their garages and sheds. No matter how obscure
the piece, Ken and Joy worked it into their creations.

One found item could inspire an entire sculpture: A shovel became a
shoulder, a log carrier became a horse's saddle.

"Somebody gave me that, and that's how I got started on the horse,"
Ken said as he led me on a tour of the gallery. "I just started laying out
pieces and seeing how they would go together."

The horse got his hooves when Ken found several engine pistons in a
scrapyard. Between the pistons and the equine's ribbons of scrap-metal
mane are flywheels, a garden rake head, tin snips, dozens of wrenches, and
a spoon his wife discarded.

Joy said a frame of sheet metal and bolts undergird the creation, which
was Ken's first after his father-in-law taught him how to use an electric
welder.

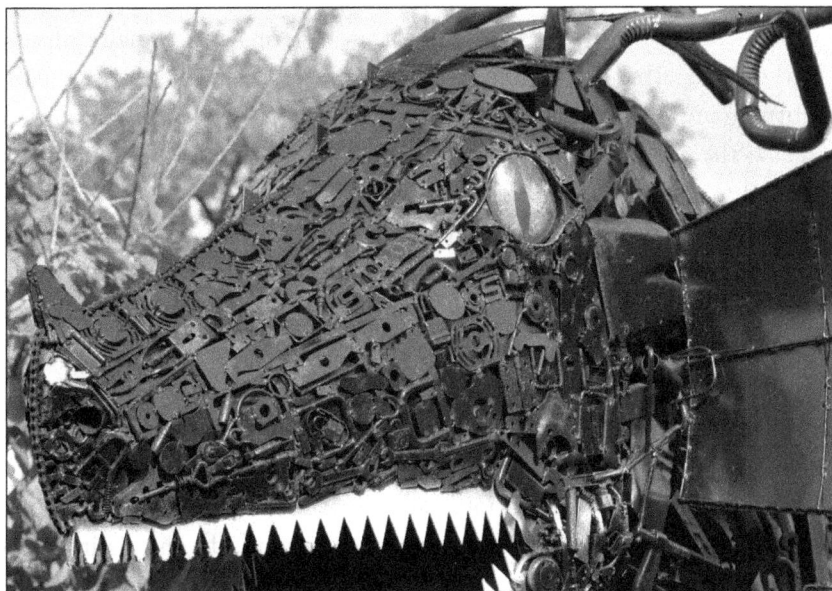

Close inspection of the dragon's head reveals the myriad metal items and shapes that go into these bigger-than-life sculptures.

"Carl Quinn of New Manchester," Ken said. "He had been a certified welder for 35 years, but he was getting sick and talked me into buying (the welder). I'd been a woodworker for as long as I can remember, and he taught me how to weld."

Ken practiced on pieces of scrap and was soon creating shapes and figures from found materials. A short time after beginning his hobby, he asked Joy to assist him by holding a piece while he welded, and she also became interested in creating junkyard art.

"Now she welds by herself," Ken said.

Her works include a scorpion, pig, flowers, and catfish. Like her father, she rarely refers to a photograph, drawing, or artist's conception. All it takes to get a project going is an unusually shaped piece of scrap that inspires the artists' imagination.

"You look at a piece, a wrench, or a saw blade—or like on the horse, a hubcap—and you think of animals that might have an anatomy like that. And then you start looking for other shapes that would (express) that anatomy," Ken said of the creative process.

Depending on what scrap resources they have on hand, a small sculpture can come together in a matter of hours. Joy saw her father work from early morning until dark when he became engrossed in a project. Other pieces, such as the dragon, required a year or more of waiting and scrounging for the right parts.

Once a week, Ken and Joy crossed the river to Steubenville, Ohio, to rummage through the industrial junkyard. Materials from defunct steel mills in the region feed the yard, where Ken found hand tools and large hardware pieces mixed in with prosaic discards.

"A lot of people will say 'How come you are using all those good tools in these things?'" Ken said. "But I got my own tools, so I don't need these." Among the unusual tools Ken and Joy have committed to the sculptures is a Model T wrench and various gauges and precision-machining tools.

Ken said they rarely cut a custom shape or modify an existing piece to make it fit. They preferred to work with the natural curves and angles of the scrap as they find it. Everything from a gasoline-pump nozzle to kitchen-knife blades, from car springs to an engine's oil pan, contributed to the creations.

The gallery was organic and evolving. At one point it had an alien and flying saucer, but a medieval theme has dominated the display since Ken made the dragon, knight, horse, and castle-wall sculptures. He trimmed the top of the hedge at an angle to reinforce the sculptures' theme.

There remained a secondary theme of alien life. Standing next to the knight was a science fiction alien with a smaller alien emerging from his chest and peering through a pair of rusty binoculars. The alien held a laser gun whose components included a motorcycle muffler and engine crankshaft.

Ken and Joy sell their sculptures, so the gallery's content fluctuates. Ken and Joy also do commissioned pieces, some of which are displayed in parks around the New Cumberland area.

Their creativity is still ignited whenever they pull into their driveway and discover a box or bucket of rusty scrap or have a productive day scrounging around a scrapyard.

"A lot of people tell me they like it," Ken said. "And that's what keeps me going."

George Farnham with a few of his bigger-than-life fiberglass figures, 2007.

Unger's character farm

Located in the Eastern Panhandle town of Unger, about 3/10 of a mile from the Virginia border, is what may be the nation's largest privately held collection of fiberglass advertising figures.

A 19-foot-tall Santa Claus, arm extended, waves to motorists on the Winchester Grade Road as they approach the George and Pam Farnham farm. In the backyard is a row of classic advertising behemoths: a beach boy holding a can of soda, the famous Muffler Man, "Big John" with arms full of grocery bags, and another Santa Claus. The figures range in height from 21 to 26 feet.

If an item was too short for the display, George mounted it on a pole. A pterodactyl and an eagle, each with a 12-foot wingspan, soared above the yard on metal poles.

"(The pterodactyl) used to rotate on a pole until it hit the neighbor's roof and he wasn't happy about that," George told me during a tour of their farm in May 2007.

Smaller fiberglass figures in this impressive collection included crabs from Baltimore, an apple from Winchester, a whale, shark, and Yogi Bear.

George moved to the Eastern Panhandle's Morgan County in 1984. He was 30 at the time and a Washington D.C. lawyer specializing in public-issue litigation. Burned out by the Beltway grind, he chucked the law career and urban lifestyle for self-employment as an antiques and collectibles dealer in rural Morgan County. Pam, whom he married after moving to Morgan County, found the farm a good place to raise alpacas.

Their first fiberglass figure, the Muffler Man, was George's 50th birthday present from Pam. A seller in California listed the 21-foot-tall figure on eBay, and Pam on the auction. Delivery was arranged as part of a moving-van's payload destined for the East Coast. Unfortunately, the trucker didn't plan his route well and packed an entire household destined for Washington, D.C., at the rear of the trailer. He failed to heed George's warning that their driveway would not accommodate the 53-foot-long behemoth.

"Thirty feet, an entire household, they had to dump in my driveway," recalled George of the day Muffler Man arrived.

On average, the fiberglass figures weigh only 300 pounds each. With the strong winds that whip across the valley, concrete footers with precisely positioned bolts are required to secure the characters. A contractor incorrectly measured the spacing by about a ¼-inch during an installation and spent two days adjusting the bolts' alignments with a sledgehammer.

One of their Santa Claus figures came from Maine, another from Texas. Big John formerly watched over a small-town supermarket in southern Illinois. The Beach Boy figure came from an amusement park and arrived in two pieces on a flatbed trailer.

An eagle, sourced from North Carolina, was the only figure George and Pam had hauled themselves. "That was the most frightening drive of my life," recalled George, who hauled it in a pickup truck. "I had one wing six feet above the cab of the truck facing the wind going down I-95. My main fear was the wing breaking off and flying through a windshield of a vehicle behind me."

They follow auction listings and depend upon a network of dealers familiar with their collecting niche. Some figures have come from collectors forced to dispose of a character because its presence violates the residential zoning code.

The huge Santa in the Farnhams' yard ensured it was always Christmas there.

No such regulations existed in Unger, which was surrounded by farmland and relatively untouched by urban sprawl when George relocated there. Ironically, a few years later, Unger's relatively permissive code opened the door to a proposed housing development that rankled the Farnhams and other former captives of suburban sprawl. The development would have transformed a 100-acre working farm into a residential community visible from the Farnhams' property. George and Pam objected to the development because it would bring more traffic on their road, require an expansion of utility and municipal services, and place additional demands on the area's natural resources. They organized like-minded residents into a protest and selected a once ubiquitous building as a symbol of their effort, the outhouse.

"Our primary issue is our fear of having our water taken away" George said. "We chose the outhouse because we are afraid that's where we are all going to end up if our wells go dry."

The protesters built nearly 100 fake outhouses from plywood, painted them in bold colors, embellished them with slogans, and planted them near the proposed site. Creative incarnations included a double-decker,

The Farnhams and like-minded Morgan County residents who resisted residential development and the public sewers that would come with them used the outhouse as an expression of their disdain in 2006. Dozens of the structures made
from plywood and placed throughout the county drew attention to their protest.

blue-and-pink, his-and-her outhouse. Another fancy outhouse had a book
slot on one side. All of them bore the message "Keep Morgan County Rural."

The protest drew media attention from Washington, D.C., Pittsburgh,
and local outlets. It also started the ball rolling on zoning regulations that
would prevent Morgan County from becoming one more suburb for
Winchester, Virginia, or Washington, D.C.

The campaign worked. In the November 2006 election, voters elected
a Democratic pro-zoning county commissioner, Brenda Hutchinson.
"Democratic candidates are never elected (in Morgan County)," George
said. "It really sent shock waves through the community. . . . we were told
we didn't have a chance of winning, and we won in a landslide."

One by one, the plywood Outhouses of Unger disappeared from the
landscape, often the victims of vandalism or theft. But George's and Pam's
bigger-than-life characters remain, as do less-political manifestations of
their protest symbol of choice, the fading privy.

Along the Way: The Old Privy

Walking around Parsons, Tucker County, during one of my first wanderings back in the late 1970s, I came across this backyard, deluxe privy that catered to both sexes. The addition of some tar-paper shingles further elevated its status among the necessary structures.

Scattered across the West Virginia landscape are survivors of that once-ubiquitous backyard necessity—the privy or outhouse.

Some owners have dolled up their artifacts to create a piece of rustic lawn art or something more practical, like a garden or tool shed. Others have allowed nature to have its way with the old house out back, but there's no mistaking the heritage of these leaning artifacts. Privy-diggers seek the location of former "pits" and excavate them for treasures that were discarded down the hole generations ago (the outhouse pits were household trash receptacles, thus old bottles and tools often turn up in the excavations). A few churches with a limited budget or unavailability of a water supply still have the restrooms "out back," which, I would guess, might impact church attendance more than the color of carpet or style of worship.

Hillbilly Haven, an outdoor music park at Morris Run, Wetzel County, made use of a Depression-era term to identify its unisex privy. The park opened in 1998 and was operated by Jack and Louise Morris.

When I was a child in the 1950s and 1960s, my maternal grandparents still maintained a privy, although a few years earlier they had become sufficiently wealthy to add an indoor facility to the back of their simple house. I still recall a little redwood plaque on the wall next to the toilet with a receptacle for change. It urged users to donate a dime for use of the amenity because moving the outhouse indoors had cost them a lot of money.

We take our conveniences for granted, but I am grateful that my childhood experiences include memories of using an outdoor privy and ripping

Located in the Northern Panhandle between Route 2 and the railroad tracks that parallel the Ohio River, this outhouse, home, and one-room schoolhouse were abandoned years before I made the image in 2004.

out a few Sears Roebuck catalog pages for toilet paper. I think my cousins and I used the outdoor option simply because it was such a novelty. I still recall the summer in the mid-1960s when my father and uncle assisted my grandfather in pulling down the old outhouse and filling in the hole.

It was the end of an era.

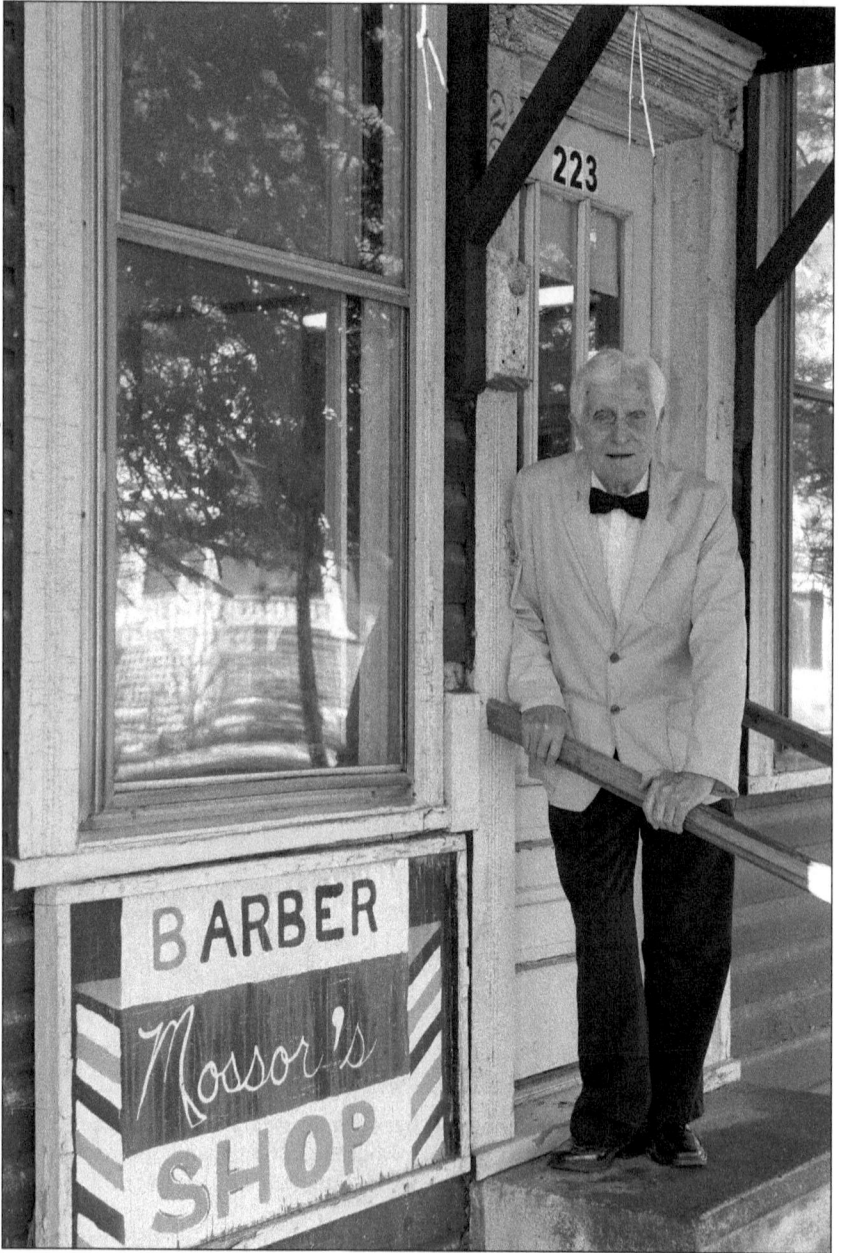

Ray Mossor, 86, stands outside his New Martinsville barbershop on March 22, 2010. Ray had been cutting hair in the Northern Panhandle for more than 50 years when we met at his shop at the corner of Clark and North streets.

Chapter 5

The Old Barbershop

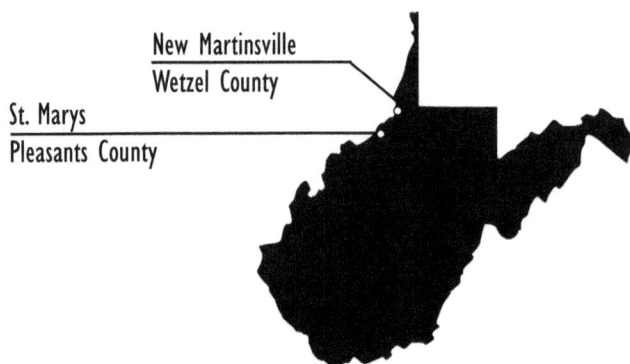

New Martinsville
Wetzel County

St. Marys
Pleasants County

The Main Street barbershop is a slice of Americana that has largely gone the way of the hometown bank, cobbler, and single-screen movie theater. Few people go to "just a barber." A stylist or beautician shampoos, cuts, and sculpts our hair. The work is done in a bright, hip salon, not a old-time barbershop. And the prices! A haircut that once set you back a hour's wage is three times that or more, plus a generous tip.

Nevertheless, in the early 20th-century there was still a barbershop that offered a gentleman's haircut for $6. That place was Ray B. Mossor's in New Martinsville.

"I don't like to rob people," said Ray, who'd been cutting hair in the Northern Panhandle for over 50 years when we spoke in 2010. A resident of Sistersville, Ray had barbered in a small, red building at the corner of Clark and North streets since 1962, when he and Ray Potts relocated their shop from Main Street. Ray bought out his former boss in 1974, and he had worked solo ever since.

The shop had changed little in appearance since the day he and Potts made their first rent payment to Wells Eakin, who was still Ray's landlord

Ray Mossor believed in proper attire befitting his profession. He always wore a black tie to his job as an independent barber.

in 2010. Ray told me that the simple structure, reminiscent of a child's playhouse, originated as a law office and was later converted to an efficiency residence. Folks told Ray that they had lived in the little building when they were first married; the main room measured 12 by 16 feet and, at one time, had been divided into a living room/bedroom. A small kitchen/bath was at the rear.

A boxy gas space heater, a wall of mirrors, two antique barber chairs, a row of waiting chairs, magazine rack, and cash register whose keys topped out at $1 occupied the barbering area. There was no television or telephone. Any form of electronic communication would be an unnecessary, unwelcome intrusion into this oasis of male conversation, the topics of which ranged from church dinners and gardening to politics and community members, both living and departed.

A native of the Tyler County hamlet of Wick, Ray was born in 1924 and grew up on a family farm. He had four brothers and two sisters, but he and his twin sister Bernice were all that remained.

His older brother, Frank, took an interest in barbering and performed

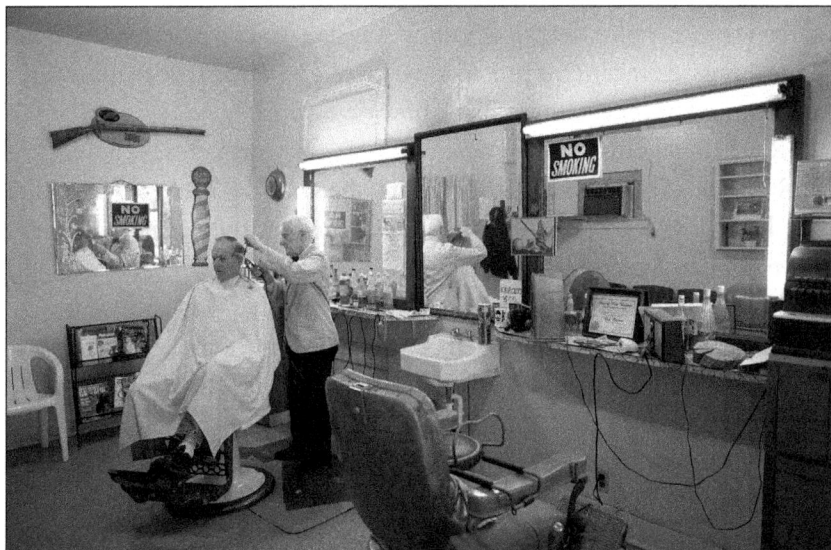

Ray Mossor was charging just $6 for a haircut in March 2010, when I visited his shop in New Martinsville. His was the only barbershop I've been in with a firearm hanging on the wall. I forgot to ask him if he used it to enforce the "no smoking" policy

the service for his four brothers and some neighbor boys. When Frank headed off to war, Ray assumed the role. After high school, Ray went to work at a Jeannette, Pennsylvania, glass factory, saved his money and, in 1946, enrolled in the Moler Barber College in Charleston.

He graduated on a Friday in July 1947 and went to work as an apprentice under Sistersville barber Ralph Fox the following Monday. Fox told Ray to treat his customer the way he wanted to be treated, and Ray followed the advice throughout his career.

Ray worked 12 years for Fox before casting his lot with Ray Potts in 1959. He said that the now-defunct Ormet aluminum plant was under construction across the river from New Martinsville, and Potts had a shop on the lower level of a downtown bank building—we'll visit that shop next. There was a ferry landing near the shop, and men waiting for the ferry killed time by getting a haircut and/or shave. Ray said they had late hours on Saturday nights to accommodate all the workers who came to town.

He recalled seven barbers in Sistersville when he started working there and about as many in New Martinsville. In 2010, it was just down to Ray and one other—plus the pricey salons. Ray had issues with salon prices and hairdressers' disregard for professional dress. He stayed true to his training and insisted upon wearing a black bow tie to work.

Ray had held his price for a haircut at $5 for years before finally hiking it by a buck. "I doubt if I'll raise it again," he said. "I got a lot of customers I've had for years. I know that price is cheap, but they usually give me a tip, especially around Christmas."

His oldest customer was Orie Welch, in his mid-90s and a customer for about as long as Ray had been cutting hair. Some of his customers first started with him when he was barbering in Sistersville. Customers were faithful and helpful.

"I got one preacher who comes in here every Friday morning," Ray said. "Frank Conley. He comes in and if it's snowing, he gets the snow shovel out and clears the path."

Ray and his wife, Nancy Givens, were married in 1954. They had five children, seven grandchildren and one great-grandchild in 2010, but none followed the barber trade.

Nancy, 11 years younger than Ray, worked for the school system, so Ray just kept on working, too. Even after Nancy retired, he couldn't walk away from his career and all the friends he's made over the years.

"I'm not going to retire as long as I can walk," he said. "I never want to retire. I can't sit on the couch and watch TV. If a person keeps busy, it's the best thing."

Barber in a bank

Farther down the Ohio River from New Martinsville, Mark Bailey performed his tonsorial services in space rented from Union Bank at the corner of Second and Washington streets, St. Marys.

The shop is located down a flight of 10 concrete steps off the Washington Street sidewalk. A barber pole and white globe identified the location. No further signage was necessary, for the shop is as much of a landmark as the railroad tracks that run down the middle of Second Street.

Mark had been the barber of record here since 1986. He rented the space from Union Bank, which owned the two-story sandstone building that rises above the basement. To the best of Mark's knowledge, a barbershop

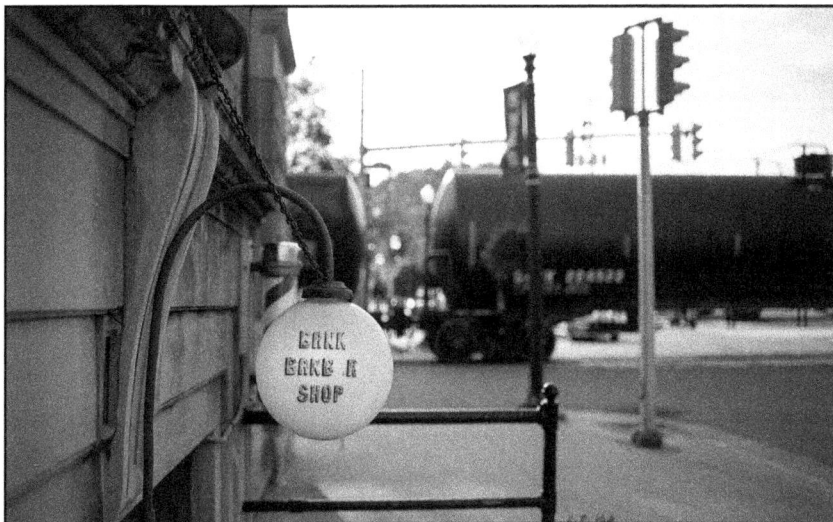

St Marys on the Ohio River is unique among West Virginia towns for the CSX Railroad tracks that run down the center of Second Street through the business district. It also has a barbershop in the basement of the bank building. Banks once hosted these shops as a convenient service for their commercial customers. The basement location of the St. Marys' shop made it susceptible to flooding from the river.

has occupied this space ever since the First National Bank building was built more than a century ago.

"I think (having a barber on site) was a kind of service that banks looked favorably upon providing their customers," said Mark, a native of St. Marys.

Mark's family did not patronize the Bank Barbershop when he was growing up, but he knows that Harold Elder was cutting hair there before Mark was born. And Elder was the barber that Mark took it over from in 1986.

"When the old barber passed away, the bank's president called me and asked if I would be interested in coming in," Mark said.

There was room for at least three chairs in the Bank Barbershop, but Mark limited the operation to his chair and the one that Marla Montgomery rented from him. Mark and Marla were the only barbers in St. Marys, although there were beauticians. Male customers accounted for about two-thirds of the shop's traffic, and Mark took care of most of them. Marla frequently cut ladies' hair, as well as that of teen boys. The stuck to the basics.

"I'm a barber," said Marla, a Williamstown resident. "I don't do any chemical treatments, no perms or colors, just haircuts."

She and Mark went to the same barber college and their paths crossed at Your Father's Moustache in the late 1970s. Mark ended up back in his hometown and four years after setting up shop in the bank's basement, he tracked down Marla to see if she was interested in joining him.

She's worked there ever since.

"This community has been good to me," she said. Like her counterpart farther up the river, Marla could not imagine retiring. "Retirement is something barbers just don't think about," she said.

Marla decorated her booth with a wall map of the world, but the front part of the shop was classic decor. A bulletin board hung near an antique shoeshine chair that had been a fixture of the shop for decades (shoeshines not offered). There was a wood-burning stove strictly for decorative purposes. A checkerboard was on a table next to it, and Mark said he had some customers, often a father and son, who engaged in a game or two while waiting.

"It's the only time they will interact with each other in a way that is not electronic," Mark said.

A small television was in the waiting area, which was stocked with magazines and classic oak furniture purchased from the bank when it modernized its décor. The room's oak trim and tire floor were original. Mark said vinyl flooring had concealed the tile for years. In the process of cleaning up after a flood, the tile was revealed and restored to its former glory.

Floods are a way of life for residents and business of this Ohio River town, and especially so for a basement barbershop. A heavy rain can send a stream down the steps and into the shop if drains become overwhelmed or clogged.

The March 1913 flood was probably the worst. Mark said the late Walter Carpenter, president of the Pleasants County Historical Society, was one of his customers and shared stories about the building's history and Ohio River floods. "The water was up to the tops of the tellers' desks," Mark said, recalling one of Carpenter's stories.

More recent floods have played havoc with Mark's livelihood, but the bank always cleaned up the mess and restored the shop for him after an

A shoe-shine station was still in place at St Marys' Bank Barbershop on Second Street.

event. "We had to go to a beauty shop in town and work out of there for a while," Mark said, recalling a flood in the fall of 2004 that sent the shop packing. "We had time to get our equipment out."

Mark said business was steady throughout the years; he raised a family on the money he made cutting hair. An adult haircut was just $9, and the most expensive service, shampoo, cut, and styling was $14.

"We haven't raised prices here in many years, 2004, I think," Mark said. "We like to starve."

Wilma Shriver stands on the horseshoe court where her late husband, a state champion, spent many carefree hours honing his pitch. She had a man paint his initial and surname on the barns so guests could easily find their farm.

Chapter 6

The Old Red Barn

Wana
Monongalia County

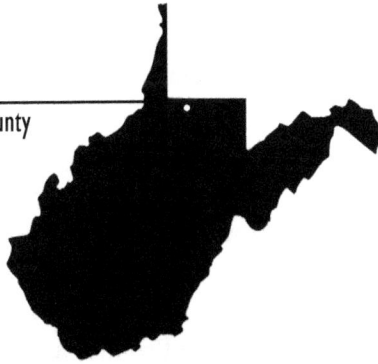

The big, red barn is disappearing from the West Virginia countryside as farming in The Mountain State shifts to big business and hardy cattle breeds. Many of the old barns that remain hold only memories of deceased husbands and their fathers and grandfathers.

Wilma Shriver's barns on Route 7 in Monongalia County were in this phase of their lives when I visited her in 2005. Finding her place was easy. Decades earlier, Wilma hired a man to paint "H. SHRIVER" in big white letters on the two red barns that face the highway. The "H" stands for Solomon Howard Shriver (also known as "Gouge"), her late husband, who died August 10, 1973, two days shy of his 59th birthday. It also could stand for "Henry D.," Howard's father, or Solomon Howard, his grandfather, or Howard Arnet, their son, who lived in the house up Wise Run Road that overlooked the farm.

Wilma had the family name painted on the barns because she got a lot of visitors who needed directions to the farm. Folks from Wilma's church, West Warren Baptist, came to Wilma's home for chili suppers and Sunday afternoon visits. Out-of-state relatives took the byways so they could make a detour to Wilma's when passing through. And kin gathered for the annual family reunion at the Shriver farm.

The farm played a role in protecting democracy, as well. Some 200 Monongalia Precinct 40 voters cast their votes there because it was a convenient polling location. Votes had been recorded in the 30-by-30-foot steel garage since the early 1980s, Wilma guessed.

"Time goes by so quickly," she said, trying to recall exactly.

A county clerk's office worker told me in 2005 that the farm was being used as a polling place when she started her job 23 years earlier. Wilma said Precinct 40 voters formerly cast their ballots in Wana, but after that building was razed, only a church remained as an option. The congregation was divided on the issue of making their building a house of worship one of democracy, as well. Wilma had just put up a new garage, and a local election official asked her if she'd mind hosting the election.

"I had no reason to say no, and they've voted there ever since," Wilma said.

Ironically, until the General Election of 2004 and redistricting of the precinct, Wilma's farm was outside Precinct 40. "Always before, we had to go to Wadestown," she said. "(In 2004), they brought me back to this precinct."

She paid $75 for the use of her garage, but Wilma said she would have provided the service to her community, regardless. "I'm just glad to have them," she said. "You know, money doesn't mean anything."

What mattered were the friends and neighbors who came by on Election Day and the camaraderie of the five election workers during the 14 hours they spent in the heated garage. When she had her new house built in 1996, Wilma selected a design with a restroom right off the back entrance so voters and workers wouldn't have to walk through her house to take care of business.

If she was feeling up to it, Wilma cooked a pot of chili and baked a cake and several dozen cookies for the workers. A few days before the election, she gave the garage a thorough cleaning and rolled out a carpet to make the polling place a little more comfortable.

Wilma, who was legally blind, joked about how her handicap might cause her to miss some dust when she cleaned the garage prior to Election Day. "If it's there, I can't see it," she said.

Wilma Shriver opened her garage to the voters of Monongalia County Precinct 40 for many years. There was no public building in the district, so Wilma offered the garage, a handy solution since the Shriver farm was a landmark and Wilma knew the residents from her years of being the Wadestown postmaster.

Despite her positive attitude toward the disability, Wilma admitted that the day she was diagnosed with macular degeneration was one of the worst of her life. It not only meant that she would no longer be allowed to drive, but also that she would have to give up her beloved job as postmaster of Wadestown, a post she held for more than 20 years.

The little post office had 125 boxes on the rural route and another 100 patrons who got their mail at the physical location. Wilma knew them all and enjoyed serving them. Perhaps that's why she welcomed Precinct 40 voters, many of them her former postal patrons, twice a year to the H. Shriver farm.

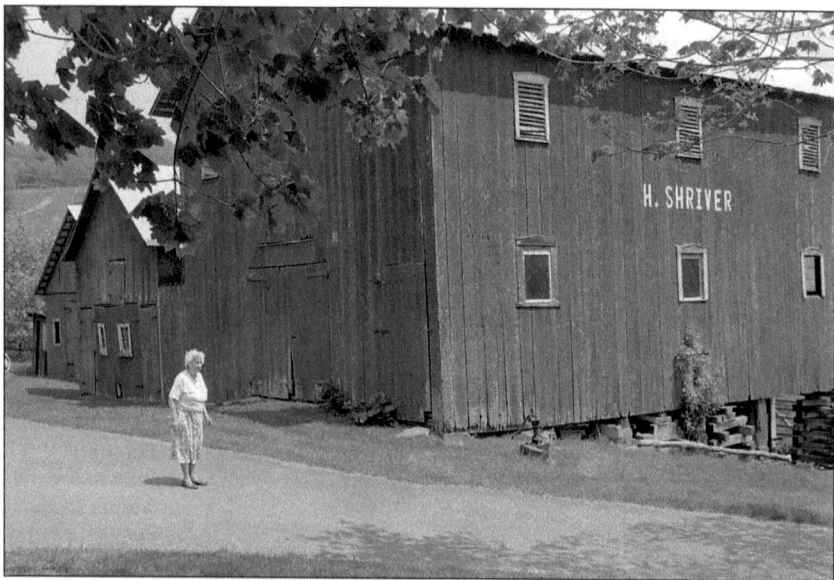

Each structure in the row of farm buildings on the Shriver farm had a function and held memories for Wilma. Her in-laws lived in the old farm "mansion" and Wilma and Howard lived in a one-room wash house by the highway after they married.

So many memories

Although Wilma saw her world dimly, vivid memories of it flourished in her mind. Each building, piece of furniture, and corner of the 243-acre farm held a story or two for her.

She prefaced those recollections by telling me that the Shrivers went way back to the 1800s in this part of the country. "At one time, when Sol Shriver was living here, there were 723 acres in this farm," she said. "Originally they raised a lot of grain here, but by the time I came along, it was sheep and cattle."

That was the farm's status in 1931, when she and Howard, both graduates of Wadestown High School, married and settled into farm life. Wilma said Howard's parents lived in the old farmhouse, or "mansion," when she and Howard married. There was a one-room wash house out by the highway, and it was in that building that Howard and Wilma started their years of marriage.

"We had a folding bed in there," she said. "It was a fine piece of furniture. You pulled it out and it made into a double bed. I wish I had it back."

The only other furnishings in the house were a baby bed, cook stove, and table-and-chairs set that her father purchased for them as a gift. Linoleum covered the floor; a fireplace with a solid slab of stone provided heat.

"It was really a cozy place," she said.

The building was eventually removed, but Wilma insisted the stone be salvaged and placed on blocks near her house to make a bench. Unfortunately, the solid slab of stone cracked in the moving process, but in 2005 it was still fulfilling its dual purpose of giving rest to the legs while jogging the memory.

Like many other newlyweds of that era, Wilma and Howard faced a hardscrabble existence. "There wasn't nothing," she said. "He worked hauling mine props; he couldn't get any other work."

In 1935, Howard found work in Michigan's oil fields. For the next seven years, he and Wilma lived away from the farm. It was a lifestyle already familiar to Wilma, because her father had worked in the drilling industry, as well.

She returned to the farm in 1942, when Howard was drafted into military service. Wilma, who had only a high school education, got an emergency teaching certificate. She taught in schools around the Wana/Wadestown area until after the war ended and the certificates became invalid.

As we walked around the outside perimeter of her home, Wilma pointed out the foundation of the house in which she, Howard, and their son lived when they moved back to the farm in 1942. It was a two-room cellar that remained from the old Shriver "mansion" that had burned. They added onto the cellar to create a home for themselves, but coal mining underneath the structure eventually compromised its stability. A flood in 1995 finished it off, thanks to mining activity altering the course of a nearby creek..

"We had to tear it down," she said. "It was coming apart because of the mining going on under it."

Wilma was out of town when she learned that her home was destroyed. "My son called me and told me that the house had flooded," Wilma said. "It shocked me, but I said, 'They are still building houses.'"

Wilma's new house was a single-story manufactured home on a large basement. The house was comfortable and airy; it suited Wilma just fine. "It's home to me. I found out you don't have to have a mansion to be happy," she said.

As we stood on the porch of the house, looking out toward Route 7 and the wetlands and stream on the other side of the highway, Wilma told me the spot was one of her favorite places in the world.

"I love to sit out here," she said. "The geese and ducks nest over there, and of the morning, they are so noisy. I can sit out here and listen to them."

She said that the two-lane Route 7 was constructed through Wana in 1928, and the byway it replaced ran right behind her house. As we walked out the back door and down the driveway, the outline of the former roadbed became evident. It explained why the row of interconnected, frame farm buildings—a barn, grain house and garage—open toward the old highway rather than Route 7 and an old hand pump was at the corner of the barn near the former byway. Wilma said the pump connected to a 90-foot-deep well, which once supplied water to thirsty travelers and their horses as they traveled the old route. The well also supplied water to the Hampshire sheep that she and her husband raised after the war.

We walked the old road until we were impeded by a fence enclosing a pasture to the east of her home and the row of farm buildings. We paused at a clearing between the last building and the fence. I could tell the spot was special to her—it is where Wilma and Howard buried Lutie. Lutie was a shepherd mix, named after the man, a Mr. Luther, who gave them the dog when their son was a lad. Lutie and Howard Arnet grew up together, but about the time Howard was graduating from high school, Lutie died.

"He always said that took the joy out of his graduation," Wilma said.

In the field beyond the fence stood the farm's big red barn with "H. SHRIVER" painted on its front. Wilma said it was the oldest of the farm buildings, constructed in the 1800s using post-and-beam construction. It cost $93 to build back then.

We passed a row of red buildings as we walked back to the house. Sheep were housed in one of the buildings, their wool was held in another until it was taken to market. The barn was being used for storage, mostly outdated equipment and stuff that was no longer useful or needed. Among those items was a homemade device used for filling burlap sacks with wool. It could be dismantled for its lumber, but Wilma wasn't ready to part with it.

Wilma apologized for the clutter in the barn but wanted me to peek inside because it held items that would illuminate the farm's story. Among the dust and clutter was a stack of walnut lumber awaiting a craftsman to

A stall in one of the barns still held horseshoes that Howard Shriver enjoyed pitching on both his court and in competitions throughout the state. Although Wilma's eyesight was failing, she could still point out details such as this from the memory of living and working on the farm with her husband and his parents for decades..

turn it into kitchen cabinets or furniture. The lumber came from a single English walnut tree that stood in their front yard. According to family lore, Sol Shriver ordered the tree and planted it, but it never bore nuts. For decades, however, it provided shade and was yet another landmark along the predecessor to Route 7.

"We had to take it down to get the house in here," Wilma said. Her son decided to have it milled into lumber for furniture, but a busy schedule and physical problems preserved this piece of family history in its raw form.

As we left the area where the lumber was stacked, Wilma pointed out a row of horseshoes hanging over a stall wall. The custom-made shoes were used by her husband in his favorite pastime. Howard pitched horseshoes all over the region and was a state champion.

"He pitched all his life," she said. "Out of 100 shoes, he'd be in the

An old pump on the Shriver farm once provided thirsty travelers and their horses and livestock with a gush of fresh water.

upper 90s. He'd do it on and on. After the day's work was done, he was out there on his court."

The horseshoe court was our last stop on the tour. Wilma said Howard, who had a heart condition, died while sitting in a chair at one end of the court. That makes this little strip of land especially bittersweet for Wilma, obviously lost in her memories as she walked its familiar course.

"I used to keep it up in pretty good shape," she said. "I felt I was doing it for him. But anymore, I just have the memory."

Wilma Rose Steel Shriver lived another 10 years after our interview; she passed August 11, 2015. Monongalia County Precinct 40 now votes at the Mason-Dixon Elementary School. The Shriver farm is home to Shriver Farm Supply

Along the Way: Mail Pouch Barns

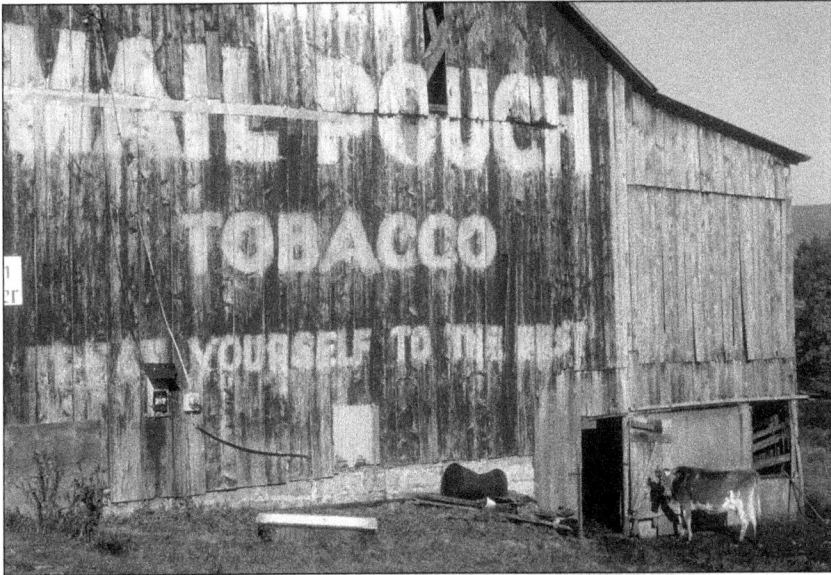

The Mail Pouch sign on this barn along Route 50 in Aurora, Preston County, was already fading back in 1982, when I made this photograph. The Wheeling tobacco company's messages were common on barns whose sides faced busy byways.

O nce a staple of the rural West Virginia landscape, the Mail Pouch Barn has become about as rare as a crossroads community without a Dollar General store.

The advertising slogan "Chew Mail Pouch Tobacco Treat Yourself to the Best," was aimed at rural customers, thus barns and other outdoor buildings with a byway-facing side made for good billboards. It has been estimated that 4,000 of these messages were painted between the early 1900s and 1992. The program was started by the Block Brothers Tobacco Company of Wheeling to promote their chewing tobacco to rural residents.

It was a good deal for the structure's owner, who got a free paint job and an annual rent payment from the company. "Space men" hired by Block Brothers scouted high-visibility locations for the signage. Contract painters applied the black background and red and white lettering.

Harley Warrick, said to have painted some 20,000 signs in his lifetime,

Block Brothers also took advantage of brick commercial building walls on which to promote their tobacco. This one was on the back of the Sutton Theater in Thomas, Tucker County.

was the last of these painters. Harley, a Belmont, Ohio, resident even did a clapboard wall inside the West Virginia State Museum in Charleston in 1976. Two years earlier, Congress had designated the signs as National Historic Landmarks.

Advertising for chewing tobacco also targeted coal miners, with an example of this being on the backside of the Cottrill Opera House, later Sutton Theater, in Thomas.

Public health's war on tobacco use, Lady Bird Johnson's disdain for outdoor advertising, and more effective advertising options eventually led the Wheeling company to stop painting new barns, although some previously painted locations were maintained. With a lifespan of 30 to 40 years, most have faded into oblivion unless the barn owner took the initiative to refresh the paint job.

It is estimated that 200 Mail Pouch signs were in West Virginia; at least eight other states in the region had them, as well.

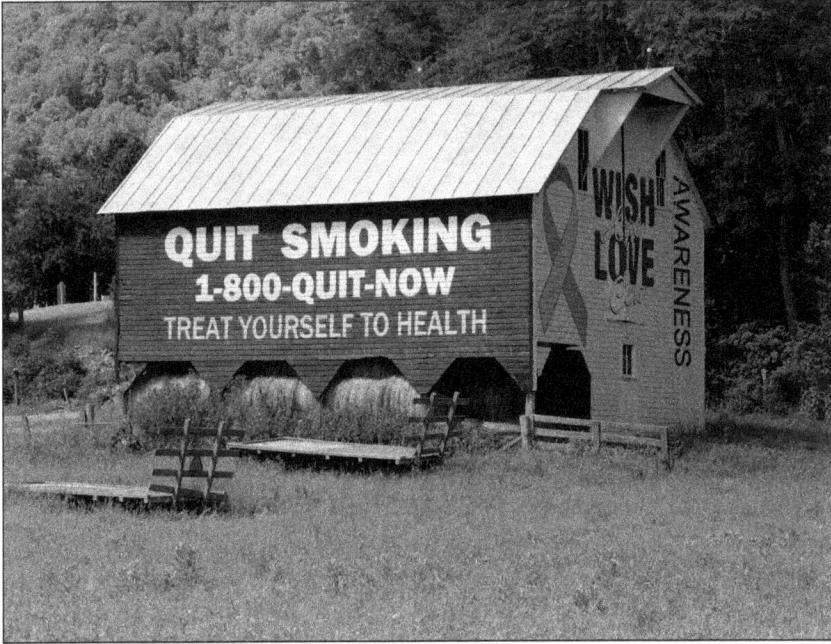

Barns still make for convenient billboards in Appalachia. This one, near Germany Valley, presented the anti-smoking message of the Centers for Disease Control and Prevention using language based upon the classic Mail Pouch message.

The practice of using barns for outdoor advertising has almost disappeared, except for those that display religious messages and political signs. Ironically, the Centers for Disease Control and Prevention uses barns to promote its anti-tobacco message and 1-800-QUIT-NOW help line. Borrowing a line from their Mail Pouch ancestor, the signs encourage citizens to "Treat Yourself to Health."

In a more artistic vein, barn owners across the United States place Americana folk art on their structures. This barn-quilt phenomenon got its start in southwest Ohio and spread throughout Appalachia and beyond. Monroe and Hardy county barn owners have been especially enthusiastic about the concept and have established formal barn quilt trails.

Cook's Mill on Route 122 in Monroe County is a lovely, accessible, restored mill nestled in a scenic setting.

Chapter 7

The Old Mill

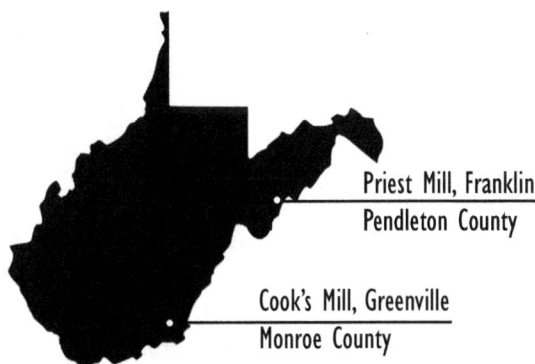

Priest Mill, Franklin
Pendleton County

Cook's Mill, Greenville
Monroe County

The gristmill, once a ubiquitous necessity on the rural landscape, has become rarer than a freshly painted Mail Pouch message. During my wanderings I have interviewed the owners of several such mills, including the last mill to grind buckwheat in Preston County (see the *Wandering Preston County* volume for that story), Reed's Mill (the first volume of the series), and Cook's and Priest mills.

Of all the mills I visited, Cook's is the loveliest and most accessible. Indeed, if the Monroe County mill were on a major highway, perhaps Route 219 rather than the little-traveled Route 122, its owners Fred and Barbara Ziegler could operate it as a bed and breakfast or rustic resort. Unfortunately, the landmark has back-roads status, a liability that hurts its income-producing potential.

Cook's Mill is a grand example of the once-abundant free-access, private roadside attractions in the state. Visitors are welcome to wander the grounds and take photographs of the bucolic scene. All Fred and Barbara ask of their guests is that they leave nothing behind and take nothing away except photographs and memories.

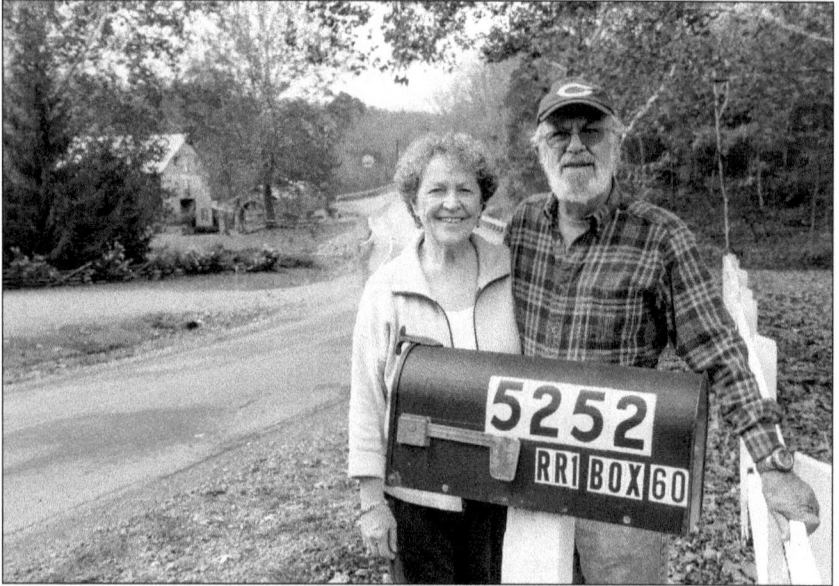

Fred and Barbara Zeigler stand outside their home on Route 122 in Monroe County. Their Cook's Mill is in the background.

Fred said most visitors honor those simple rules and show respect for the couple's grist mill/retirement project.

The 1857 mill drew the couple from their home in Chicago to Greenville in 2003, after Fred retired as a geology professor at the University of Chicago. They learned about the property from the esoteric publication of The Society for the Preservation of Old Mills (spoom.org), which published a quarterly magazine. Jim Wells was seeking a buyer for his Cook's Mill, which he had owned since 1987. And the Zieglers were in the market for one.

"My brother had owned one since 1975," Fred said. "We looked at nine different mill properties, from New Hampshire to West Virginia. This one was attractive for us for a lot of reasons . . . and we have relatives in the area."

Fred, a Massachusetts native, and Barbara, from Michigan, had little difficulty adapting to the rural lifestyle of Monroe County. The task of continuing Jim Well's renovation and preservation work was familiar to them. The couple had rehabilitated century homes in Chicago, and Fred is a skilled woodworker.

The mill and its setting rival that of Babcock State Park. Many photographers prefer Cook's Mill because there are fewer competing photographers to shoot around and there are many angles from which to photograph it.

"I'm also interested in alternative energy, which comes with the mill," he told me during my visit in 2016.

The couple moved to the property in 2003. The first big project was a renovation and expansion of the miller's home, which stands across the highway from the mill property. Fred said that it was standard and essential that the miller's home be close to the mill. The mill owner's home is extant, as well, and about a mile up the valley.

The Zieglers built an addition to the back of the original house using post-and-beam construction. At one end of this room stands a clay fireplace that mimics the fossil seabed Fred studied for his doctorate, right down to the tracks left by an ancient salamander. At the opposite end, an elaborate wood railing on the balcony fuses Gothic and Romanesque arches, architecture Fred experienced while living in England. Below the railing, which was turned by Fred, the massive beam bears the inscription, "Happy is the house that shelters a friend."

The stream that feeds the mill pond rises behind the house and becomes

Fred Zeigler looks out at the dam and millpond from a mill window, 2016.

Indian Creek after flowing under the highway and through the mill property. The source of water explains the mill's siting.

A restored log cabin, maintained as a guesthouse for family and friends, stands near the mill pond and opposite the mill. A water wheel on a row of buildings that face the mill is confusing. Fred said the wheel has nothing to do with Cook's Mill, which is powered by a vertical turbine.

"It was totally token," Fred said of the nonfunctional wheel. "It came from another structure that was about to fall down; the wheel was just there for decoration."

The creek supplies water to the millpond, the drop from which would power the vertical turbine. The pond is essential and a maintenance headache. Every 25 to 30 years, the mill owner must dredge all the organic matter and dirt that accumulates there. The biggest challenge is to find a place to put the dredged muck—it needs to dry out for at least a year before it can be used.

Such are the pragmatic challenges to owning a mill property, even an idle one. Maintaining the property is enough to keep several people busy; the Zieglers employed a handyman to assist them and contract out big tasks.

The mill pond reflects Cook's Mill, which was not operating in 2016. Removing the accumulation of muck in the pond is a major maintenance challenge.

As owners and stewards of the historically significant site, the couple felt an obligation to make it accessible. It is a popular site for weddings and a favorite setting for portrait sessions. Landscape photographers love it, many of them even more so than the iconic Babcock State Park Mill because there is less competition with other photographers seeking that perfect shot.

The owners even provide a parking lot for visitors. "The previous owner explained to me that there is no way to keep people out, and you can't build fences around it," Fred said.

Fred researched the mill's history and discovered that their inability to monetize the investment is consistent with the property's heritage.

"This mill has gone belly up probably a half-dozen times," he said. "I have found notices where it was to be sold at the courthouse steps for back taxes, and sometimes it was (repurchased) by the same guy, at a lower figure than the debt."

For more information about visiting the mill, visit the website first, cooksoldmill.com.

Along the Way: Priest Mill

Vincent and Shirley Budris outside their Priest Mill, Franklin, 2011.

Vincent Budris was looking for ways to be green long before the entire nation jumped on the renewable energy bandwagon. As Vince and his wife, Shirley, were re-organizing their lives for retirement, he began searching for a vintage water-powered mill that could be modified to generate electricity for their home, which, ideally, would be adjacent to their house.

"I was a millwright and I had worked around machinery all my life," said Vince during a visit back in 2011. "I wanted something to do when I retired."

They were living in Connecticut at the time and despite expanding their search to New England, they could not find a mill for sale. Most had been torn down, turned into a museum, or otherwise re-purposed.

While visiting Shirley's relatives in Fairmont, the subject came up and a relative suggested they investigate opportunities along the South Branch of the Potomac. That referral led them to visit Franklin's Priest Mill, which was owned by Myrick and Catherine Smith at the time.

The Samuel Priest family, which was known for its woodworking skills, in 1894 built the first mill at this site to provide wood-milling services. Their machinery included a Josiah Ross wood planer that could simultaneously plane and cut the groove or tongue in lumber. Many Franklin-area homes are embellished with flooring, trim, and gingerbread finished at the Priest Mill. The machinery that planed the wood was essential to this operation and the family's financial security. When the mill caught on fire in 1899, local men risked their lives to rush into the burning building and carry out the 1,200-pound piece of equipment.

Everything else was lost, but the Priest family rebuilt the mill, which opened in 1900. The mill also had two carding machines for wool and produced both batting and roving.

In 1916, the mill took on an additional role of generating electricity to power Franklin's streetlights and the homes of several early-adopters. Eventually, the community's power needs exceeded the mill's generating capacity, and the system was retired. But the generating equipment, along with the planer and carding machines, remained secure in the mill.

"It was amazing, so much of the machinery had been left," Shirley said. There was no indication the mill was for sale, but after their visit, Shirley and Vince sent the Smiths a note saying that they would be interested if it ever came up.

That resulted in an invitation to spend the weekend with the Smiths and learn more about the mill. Before returning home, the mill owners offered to sell it to them.

"I always wanted to generate my own electricity, and when I saw that generator in there, it was like, 'Wow!'" Vince said.

Restoration proceeded slowly because Vince had several more years to work before he could retire. Relatives were recruited to help on vacations and long weekends. "My father called it the 'slave camp,'" Shirley said. The couple converted an old service building into temporary living quarters while they worked on the mill. New lap siding was installed over the mill's entire exterior; concrete walls along the raceway and the stone walls of the mill had to be rebuilt. The tasks required 200 cubic yards of concrete.

Vince also had to bring the generator, governor, and turbine back

Vince Budris checks the operation of the turbine during my visit to the mill in 2010. It was generating electricity for the couple's home.

into service. The governor, which ensures a constant rotation speed to the shaft, was particularly challenging. The manufacturer, Woodard, was still in business, and the company provided an "old-timer's" expertise and archived documentation that helped Vince return the device to a serviceable condition.

They also had to build a house, the third time they'd done so in their lives. Based on a log cabin design, the house featured frame construction with liberal use of pine that was finished on the mill's planer and other machinery powered by the waters of the South Branch. Vince also made many of the cupboards, tables, and other furniture in their home using the same equipment that is powered by the mill's electrical generator.

The system supplied about 23 kilowatts at peak water flow, more than adequate to meet all the electrical needs of their home, which was heated with electric baseboard units. Nevertheless, the house also had a connection to the grid as a backup source during times of low water, generator maintenance, or prolonged absence from home.

Keeping the water intake to the turbine clear of debris is a daily chore associated with an operating mill. Vince Budris shows uses a tool designed for the job.

A meter on a table next to Vince's living room chair indicated the system's status and alerted him to malfunctions such as a broken belt or shaft spinning too quickly or slowly.

"When the lights start dimming, you know something is wrong," Shirley said.

An old log kept by the Priest family occasionally mentioned problems with mush ice, a term unknown to Vince and Shirley until they encountered the same problem. Mush ice is globular, slushy water that will block flow to the turbine gate and reduce power output unless it is addressed.

"I found out you can't have a lot of mush ice," Vince said.

Vincent died in 2012, just several months after our interview. Privately owned, Priest Mill is on the National Register of Historic Places.

Anthony "Tony" Ellis pauses on a speaker post at his family's Sunset Drive-In back in 1994, when I first met him and Jim Henderson, who was leasing the Sunset from the Ellis family. The Sunset is the only operating drive-in in north-central West Virginia.

Chapter 8

The Old Drive-in Theater

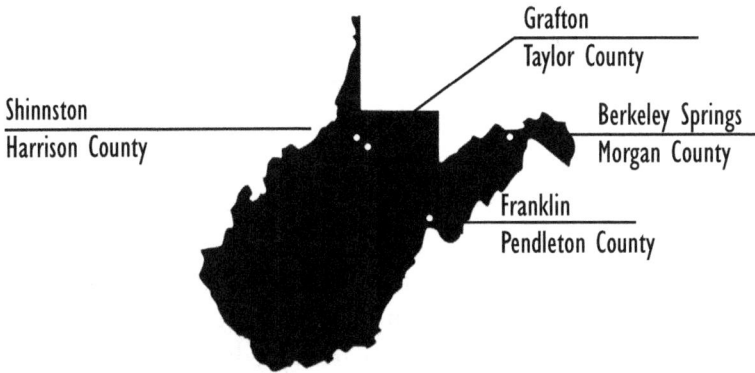

I love movies, especially the old ones, black-and-white or Technicolor, with dialog that doesn't make an old guy like me cringe with embarrassment when in the presence of my wife or teenage grandson.

Several drive-in movie theaters were within 30 minutes of my childhood home in northeast Ohio. I fondly recall those special Saturday nights watching *Ma and Pa Kettle* features and inevitably falling asleep in the backseat long before "The End" flashed on the huge screen and floodlights beamed into my lair.

I do not recall any drive-in theater experiences during our visits to relatives in West Virginia. However, I fondly recall going to the Sutton Theater in Thomas with my Aunt Barbara (Long), who was considerably younger than my mother. I remember seeing the Little Rascals and Three Stooges shorts on the Sutton screen. And I recall hearing the screaming during Alfred Hitchcock's *The Birds* as my father and I waited for Aunt Barb to come out of the picture show that I was too young to get into.

At both the drive-in and indoor shows, my favorite part of movie-going was not so much the movie itself, but the projection booth. I loved watching the dancing bean as it exited the rectangular openings behind the balcony. It was pure magic to me that this ray of light could be transformed into huge images as soon as it made contact with the screen. It was so elementary yet spellbinding; I was drawn to this light as one transitioning from this world to eternity. When my father and I went to the drive-in's concession stand, I dawdled outside the projection booth, watching the sweaty men in their white T-shirts and black pants hoist and thread 2,000-foot reels of film into the arms of the carbon-arc projectors and synchronize the switchover between machines. I often regret that, as a teenager, I did not attempt to secure a job in one of these fading movie palaces or passion pits in the early 1970s, when drive-ins and single-screen theaters alike were commencing their final fade to black.

Sunset for the Drive-ins

Drive-in operators began to experience this decline during the late 1960s. Anthony "Tony" Ellis, owner of Shinnston's Sunset Drive-In, told me that drive-ins took a huge hit from a lack of fresh product when studios adopted a policy of allocating first-run films to indoor venues only. The dearth of material was so severe, the Sunset did not open for the 1974 season despite nearly three decades of continuous operation. Thereafter, Tony booked horror, thriller, and action flicks, but refused to screen the X-rated and cult material many drive-ins relied upon to stay open. In 1978, he opened the grounds to a weekend flea market that helped pay the theater's bills.

As with all movie theaters that screened current releases, drive-in owners had to convert to digital projection when studios stopped distributing their product on 35mm film in 2013. The cost of conversion was too much for most of these mom-and-pop drive-ins that struggled to pay the operating costs and taxes, let alone raise enough capital for the $100,000-plus investment. Even running weekend flea markets and holding special events could not generate enough income to light the screen with a digital image.

The Ellis Sunset was a rare exception. The drive-in experience is so ingrained in the culture of north-central West Virginia and the Sunset so beloved by the community, a crowd-funding effort raised enough money to upgrade the system and ensure the Sunset's longevity. The most recent system funded through that effort was actually the drive-in's second digital

Built in the late 1940s by four partners, the Sunset Drive-In in Shinnston featured a number of innovations that, in theory, would have made year-around operation possible. The "Rain Visors" were designed to keep rain and snow off the vehicles, and electric heaters were on each pole and could be placed inside the car, along with the speaker, to make cold-weather drive-in attendance a possibility. The top image is from the drive-in's early days, while the lower one is from my first visit to it in 1994. In 2024, the Sunset is north-central West Virginia's last operating drive-in, having converted to digital projection through assistance from a crowd-funding project.

Top image courtesy of the drive-in owners.

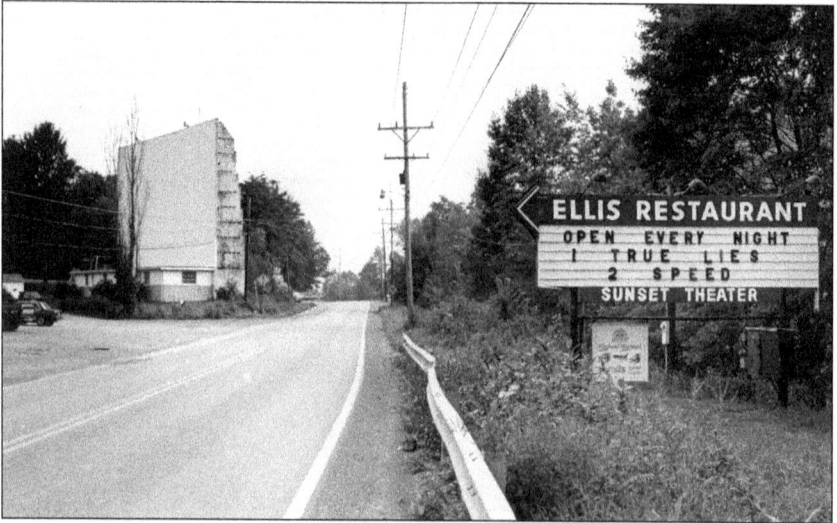

Located along Route 19 near Shinnston, the Ellis Restaurant and Sunset Theater made for a thriving business combination that served the family well for more than six decades. The restaurant closed in 2022; the drive-in remains open along with its flea market.

investment. The first, installed for the 2013 season, was damaged during a vandalism spree in January 2022. Electronics were ripped out and the projector damaged and rendered unreliable, even after repairs. The crime threatened the drive-in's survival.

"We ran fine for three days, but that's the only weekend we've operated without a hitch. The next weekend, my brother went up to start the projector and it wouldn't run. We had to turn people away and give them their money back," Tony recalled.

Concurrent with all the technical issues at the drive-in, Tony was dealing with the pain of closing the drive-in's companion Ellis Restaurant after 63 years. His parents, John and Jean Ellis, purchased the drive-in and its concession stand for $85,000 from two of the theater's original owners and builders, Alex Silay, and Steve Medve. Along with Charles Perez and Lawrence Bermejo, the men first opened the Sunset Drive-In Theater for business on August 31, 1947.

Tony said it was built on swampy farmland.

"They had no machinery to build this with. They used shovels, picks,

Jean and John Ellis (left side) serve up food to the patrons of their Sunset Drive-In in this undated/uncredited photo. The boy at the left appears to be wearing pajamas, while the woman receiving the plate appears to be dressed for a formal dinner! *Anthony Ellis collection.*

wheelbarrows, and ice tongs. That's how they got those concrete blocks for the screen up there, with ice tongs," Tony said.

The Sunset was designed for year-round use. Corrugated metal roofs on poles, termed "Rain Visors," provided cover for patron's vehicles and conceivably allowed the show to play in inclement weather. Barmejo reportedly obtained a patent on his invention, a few which remained standing long after their questionable usefulness had faded. Portable heaters that could be removed from the pole and placed inside the vehicle were provided, as well. The heaters, which operated on 220 volts, were removed in the early 1970s.

Business was terrific at the Sunset in its early years. Tony said the drive-in had 600 parking spots, and owners collected 50 cents a head. The partners were so busy on the weekends they didn't have time to count the take until Tuesdays.

The theater's location was at the end of a Clarksburg trolley line, and an old car from that line was across the highway from where the restaurant

The days of the $3.50 admission, 1994 to be exact, are long gone at the Sunset Drive-In in Shinnston, but the flea market still operates there 30 years later.

was built. The developers moved the car onto the theater property and re-purposed it as a concession stand when the line closed in 1947.

Tony said his father, who grew up in a coal camp, had but a second-grade education and could not read or write. Nevertheless, he attained the position of union president at his employer, Pittsburgh Plate and Glass.

"They had to go to Columbus every year for the contract (vote)," Tony said. "My mother (Jean, who had a sixth-grade education) would read him the whole contract on the way there, and he retained it . . . and presented it in front of everybody at that meeting, He always signed his name with an 'X.'"

John and Jean owned another restaurant as early as 1940 and purchased a Clarksburg bar/poolroom in 1945. They had the experience, reputation for good food, and clientele to start a restaurant that would complement a drive-in operation. The former trolley car/concession stand was reborn as the Ellis Restaurant in 1955.

The mom-and-pop eatery occupied the trolley car until 1960, when the structure, anchored in concrete, was demolished to make way for a larger,

Running a theater, flea market, and restaurant became too much for Anthony Ellis, who closed the Ellis Restaurant in 2022 and has since leased it to another operator. In his late 80s, Anthony continued to operate the drive-in with help from his family.

modern dining room and lunch counter. Permanent Builders designed and built the structure, which had a second story that housed a radio broadcasting booth for Clarksburg's WHAR. An advertisement for the new restaurant stated that a WHAR disc jockey would "meet and greet customers over the radio. To the rear of this broadcast booth is an open-air stage where radio talent meets and performs for the fans."

From the time he was old enough to put empty soda bottles in their wood cases, Tony worked in both businesses. Weekly compensation was 50 cents. By the time he was a teenager, he could perform virtually every task at the drive-in, including running the projectors. When a bulb burned out in a fixture atop the screen, Tony climbed up the reinforcing bars sticking out of the concrete blocks and edged his way across the top of 60-foot-tall structure to reach the faulty light bulb.

The lives and livelihoods of John Ellis's family centered around the theater and restaurant 24-hours-a-day; their living quarters were in rooms at the base of the screen: a ground-level kitchen, a bedroom on the second

The block construction of the Sunset Drive-In's screen is evident in this historical photo. The Ellis family had their living quarters at the bottom of the screen. *Anthony Ellis collection.*

floor, and two floors of storage. "My mom and dad lived in there until they passed away," Tony said.

Following graduation from high school in 1955, Tony headed off to Wheeling Jesuit University, where he earned his bachelor's in biology. He worked at the family businesses during breaks and played saxophone in dance bands. It was a chore to get from Wheeling back to Clarksburg; the bus ride took four-hours because of all the stops along the route. When he hitchhiked, Tony completed the trip in two hours, no fare required!

He worked as a biology teacher at Notre Dame High School in Clarksburg from 1962 to 1967. Tony recalled his teaching years as the most enjoyable in his work history.

"Those five years were years I will never forget," he said. "They were a very pleasurable time for me. The students in those days were respectful, helpful, and courteous. They gave me a lot of pleasure."

Despite the satisfaction he received from teaching, Tony walked away from the profession to run the restaurant and drive-in with his wife, Sue, and brother, John. The couple's daughters, Antoinette Ellis-Casto and Melissa Minigh, worked in the restaurant throughout high school and college.

Anthony Ellis, owner of the Sunset Drive-In, and Jim Henderson, who owned and operated the Grafton, stand at the Sunset in 1994. Henderson also leased and operated the Sunset from Ellis at that time.

"Melissa was a cook, Antoinette was a waitress," Tony said. "Even after they were married, before they had kids, they helped us whenever we needed them. It's still a family operation."

The Grafton

North of Grafton, on Route 119 and nestled in a farming valley, The Grafton Drive-In was one of north-central West Virginia's last operating theaters when I visited it in 1994.

Owners Jim and Mary Ruth Henderson welcomed me into their operation and gave me access to that hallowed ground of my childhood, the projection room.

The Hendersons had owned the Grafton since 1983. Located a couple of miles north of U.S. Route 50, the drive-in's fluorescent-tubed sign, 1950's style ticket booth, and 30-by-72-foot screen caught the unsuspecting

The ticket booth/entrance of the Grafton provided two windows to handle the large line of vehicles that would back up on Route 119. Image from 1994.

motorist by surprise; Eddie Murphy or Fred Flintstone performing on a hillside surrounded by farmland was just surreal.

For the Hendersons, the drive-in was both a business and their home. They lived in a house that overlooked the manicured field where gray speaker boxes bloomed on metal stalks. Mary Ruth could look out her kitchen window and watch the movie while washing dishes, but she had far more pressing duties. If she saw the movie, it was from the concession stand counter where she, their daughter-in-law, Christy, and employees Donna Myers and Amy Snyder served up mountains of popcorn and rivers of soft drinks.

Jim spent his summer nights at the Sunset Theater, which he and Mary DeAngelis of Morgantown were leasing from Tony Ellis. The Grafton and Sunset drive-ins complemented each other and were all that remained of the 25 theaters that once operated within a 20-mile radius in north-central West Virginia. Jim Henderson said the two survived because they were still making money, not because they fulfilled the owners' appetite for nostalgia.

The Grafton Drive-In's screen was set against a hillside where cattle roamed and occasionally cavorted for the distracted audience. The drive-in was owned by Jim and Mary Ruth Henderson at that time. Image from 1994.

"I like it, but if it wasn't making money, believe you me, it would be a flea market or something else," Jim said. "It would be just like all the others."

The Hendersons' tenacity in the drive-in theater business was aided by their other business ventures—The Capri Pizza Parlor, in downtown Grafton; The Manos, an indoor movie house next to The Capri; and Giovanni's, a Morgantown pizza shop they co-owned with Mary DeAngelis.

Synergy was at play. The Capri supplied pizzas for drive-in patrons and picked up the slack when the movie was rained out. The Manos opened when The Grafton closed. In April, the "closed" sign went up at The Manos and moviegoers headed north to The Grafton.

Jim bought The Grafton at a time when drive-ins were being razed in favor of parking lots, office buildings, and auto auctions. But he saw advantages in owning the only two motion picture theaters in Taylor County. Drive-ins often had to wait for a first-run film to finish playing in the indoor houses before it became available to outdoor screens. In Taylor County, Jim Henderson was his only competition.

In the winter months, the Hendersons ran the Manos Theater in downtown Grafton. A community group, Unleash Tygart, is working to re-open the East Main Street movie house as a performance and event venue. Back in the 1950s, the Manos tried to compete against the emerging threat from television by giving away bushel baskets of groceries to lucky patrons. Now, the old theaters rely upon nostalgia, live performances, and events for revival, epitomized by the diverse venues at the restored Robinson Grand in Clarksburg.

Mary DeAngelis and her husband, John, loved the drive-in theater business and owned the Grafton before the Hendersons purchased it. They also built the Blue Moon in Wellsburg and The Ohio Valley in Follansbee. All three theaters are history.

Jim's lifelong association with The Grafton and its prior owners, John and Mary DeAngelis, sealed his future in the business long before he wrote the check to purchase it. The Hendersons and the Armstrongs grew up on the same road, about a half-mile from The Grafton. Jim said the Summers family, which was associated with the Clarksburg-based Compton Coal Company, built the drive-in 1949 on farmland.

Virgis Summers operated the theater for several years, lost interest in it, and put it up for sale in 1953.

Jim had but one memory of the drive-in's early days. "I just remember that the people who had it had three beautiful girls," he said. "They always laid on top of the projection booth and got a suntan."

John and Mary DeAngelis were visiting relatives in Grafton when they noticed the drive-in was for sale. They bought it and moved to Grafton from Follansbee.

The DeAngelises were experienced drive-in theater operators/owners.

In 1949, they built the Blue Moon in Wellsburg. They sold out to their partner a couple of years later and built a second theater, The Ohio Valley, in Follansbee. Both are long gone.

"I loved the theater business, so I got my husband interested in it," Mary said during an interview in 1994. "I had just always loved that since I was a kid. I used to walk by the ticket booth of the theater and say to myself, 'I am going to own a theater someday.'"

John and Mary had just sold The Ohio Valley when they came across The Grafton. They fell in love with it and made it their home and livelihood for the next three decades. "My husband and I worked together all those years," Mary told me. "He always took care of the maintenance, and I took care of the snack bar, booking the films, and advertising."

Mary could not remember one bad year. "To me, it never was work," she said. "And for my husband, too, it never was work."

John and Mary added more parking spots and doubled the size of the screen soon after they purchased The Grafton. "At that time, Cinemascope had just come out," she said. "The big pictures were in Cinemascope, so you had to do what you had to do to get the big movies."

The theater could hold between 250 and 260 cars. Mary said there were many nights in the 1950s that patrons had to be turned away because there was no room to put their vehicles. They ran a seven-day-a-week schedule from early spring to Thanksgiving.

To encourage attendance on weekday nights, promotions like bingo games and gifts for the first 100 patrons were offered. "We had bingo once a week," Mary recalled. "That filled up the place." Prizes totaled $100 a night, plus a crack at the jackpot, which kept growing. Mary recalls it getting as high as $800 before a lucky patron won it. Mary said they gave away cigarette lighters to male patrons and strings of simulated pearls to the ladies.

Jackpots and gifts were unnecessary on weekends. The low admission, 50 cents a person, and lack of competition from television and cable made the drive-in an attractive entertainment option.

"That was cheap entertainment," Mary said. "And there was nothing else to do." It was cheap entertainment for the operator as well. Mary recalls paying only $12.50 to rent a feature film for the weekend. A cartoon added $5 to the bill.

Mary said some of the drive-in's best grossing films were those in the

The Hendersons purchased The Grafton in 1987 and lived on the property. The entire family was involved in running the show: from left, Jim and Mary Ruth, their son Jeff and his wife, Christy. The drive-in had a wide-screen that could accommodate the newer Cinemascope format, giving it a modicum of longevity compared to the boxy 4:3 screens at drive-ins whose screens were concrete block.

Ma and Pa Kettle series and flicks by Gene Autry and Elvis Presley. But the film they really had to turn people away from came in the 1970s, *The Best Little Whorehouse in Texas,* with Dolly Parton and Burt Reynolds. Clint Eastwood's *Every Which Way But Lose* and Lucille Ball's *Long, Long Trailer* also drew overflow crowds.

The images on the screen were not the only attraction for patrons. John DeAngelis pastured black Angus cattle on the verdant hills surrounding the theater. The red Mail Pouch barn he built for his livestock still stood to the north of the drive-in when I visited it in 1994. Cattle frolicked and occasionally fought on the hill above the screen, providing added entertainment for the city folk who drove down from Morgantown.

"The people who came to the drive-in just loved to watch the cows," Mary recalled. "Sometimes the bulls would get in a fight. That was a big

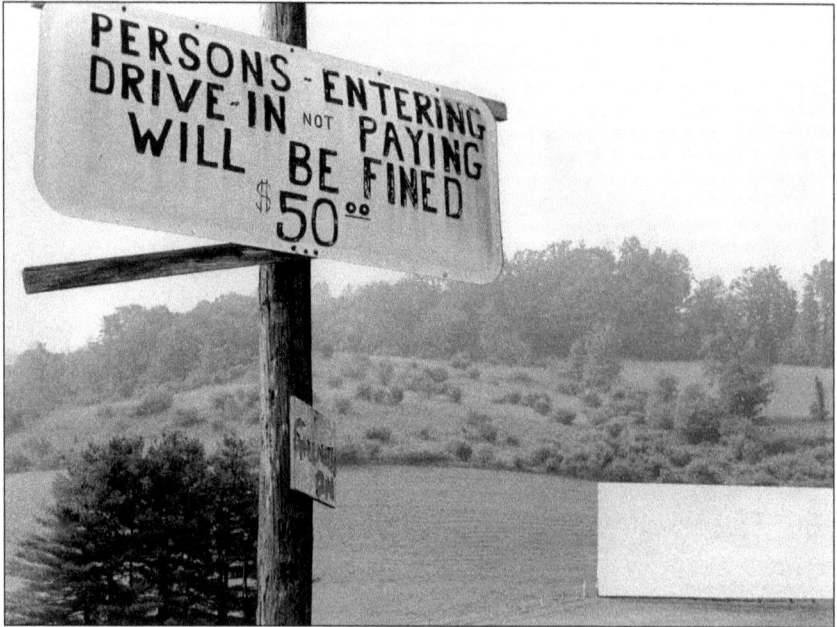

Drive-in operators often hired security workers to watch out for patrons who tried to sneak into the show via the trunk of a car or exit.

deal for them to watch that. They used to come early, spread their blankets on the field, and eat dinner there."

When the DeAngelises first purchased the theater, the concession stand was located in the basement of what became their home. They later built a separate stand from which Mary served hot dogs, chili, popcorn, and all the other drive-in goodies. Mary cooked the chili herself. People came for the food, atmosphere, and movie.

"I had people come in before the show and sit out under the trees just to eat a hot dog before the movie," Mary said.

Jim went to work for the owners when he was 11. "I was riding my bicycle down the road and the people who had just took the drive-in over asked me if I'd want to work picking up (trash). I said, 'I don't care.' They always thought that was kind of funny because I said I 'didn't care.'"

Mary Ruth was 13 when she began her career at The Grafton. She was just following in her older brother's footsteps when she took the job at the snack counter.

Mary Ruth Henderson oversaw the concession stand, where, in 1994, a small coffee was 35 cents, a hamburger or hot dog 85 cents, large soft drink $1, and the largest buttered popcorn $3.

"My oldest brother (Howard Armstrong) worked here when the original owner had it," Mary Ruth said. "They were so busy back then, they had to have the boys direct the cars in and help park them. They would take these flashlights out and direct the cars."

Junior Armstrong, another brother and projectionist at both theaters, started in the industry by making popcorn at The Grafton concession stand when he was 12 or 13.

"At that time, when you lived in the country, there was nothing else to do," Junior said. "We worked in the snack bar as soon as we were old enough to see over the bar."

Junior began apprenticing in the projection booth during the mid-1950s. As a teenager, Junior ran the 16mm projector at school, and he quickly applied that knowledge and experience to the 35mm machines at the drive-in. He kept the projectors at The Manos and Grafton in top condition; when there was no work for him in the projection booths, he helped in the pizza shop.

"My father was what they kind of called a jack of all trades and master of none," he said. "It's rubbed off on me. I kind of pick things up easily."

That was a good quality for a projectionist to have, particularly when dealing with equipment that was decades old. Junior was a one-man show when it came to the projection booth. The projectors in both the Sunset and Manos were carbon-arc illuminated Super Simplex units with a capacity of 2,000-feet of film each. Junior changed and threaded a reel at least every 20 minutes. Once the show was underway, he was confined to the booth for the evening.

The carbon arc in the doused projector was changed out while the second projector was running. Keeping an eye on the intense light was part of the job. If the gap between the rods became too large or atmospheric conditions were unfavorable, the intense light that contributed to the film's cinematic look could suddenly go out, the screen go dark, and the car horns start honking.

Friday nights were the most challenging for Junior. That's when the films got their first run. Sometimes the reels were marked incorrectly and got out of order during projection. He had reels come through with bubble gum substituted for splicing tape. Junior, and the audience, discovered the problem when it manifested itself on the screen.

If the issue could be resolved in 10 or 20 seconds, Junior hopped on it and allowed the screen to go blank. Most patrons didn't notice the interruption. But if the problem would take longer to address, Junior made an announcement through the sound system that there would be a short intermission while technical difficulties were tackled.

Such was the case when the electrical system failed in one of the two projectors at the beginning of a show. Repairing it that night was out of the question, so he made an announcement that there would be a brief pause between each reel because only one machine was operational.

"We never had a single horn blow and not one person complained," he said.

Even if horns did blow, Junior was unlikely to hear them with all the noise in the projection booth. But he did hear occasional knock at the door from a patron disgusted with the quality of the film or projection. Some people took the projectionist's challenges personally.

He recalled a particularly dark print of *The Crow* that played poorly on

Junior Armstrong, Mary Ruth Henderson's brother, was projectionist at The Grafton and Manos theaters. Each projection booth had two of these 35mm projectors that held 2,000 feet of film each, or about 18 minutes of programming. Carbon arcs provided the light source necessary for the long projection distances.

the huge outdoor screen despite cranking up the projectors' light output. "One guy came down here and wanted to take me on," Junior said. After explaining that the issue was beyond his control, the patron settled down.

"It seems like once you explain things to the people, they don't get as irate," he said.

Junior also was accused of "cutting the reels down" to shorten the movie. "This one guy dozed off and missed part of the movie," he recalled. "He came down here complaining because he thought we'd done messed it up. I said, 'You got to watch it, you can't go to sleep.'"

Falling asleep was a common problem, especially during the second feature. "You'd be surprised how many people go to sleep and we have to go around and wake them up," Junior said. He and security guard John Shingleton walked the grounds after the last film ended, knocking on windows and informing sleeping patrons that it was time to go home.

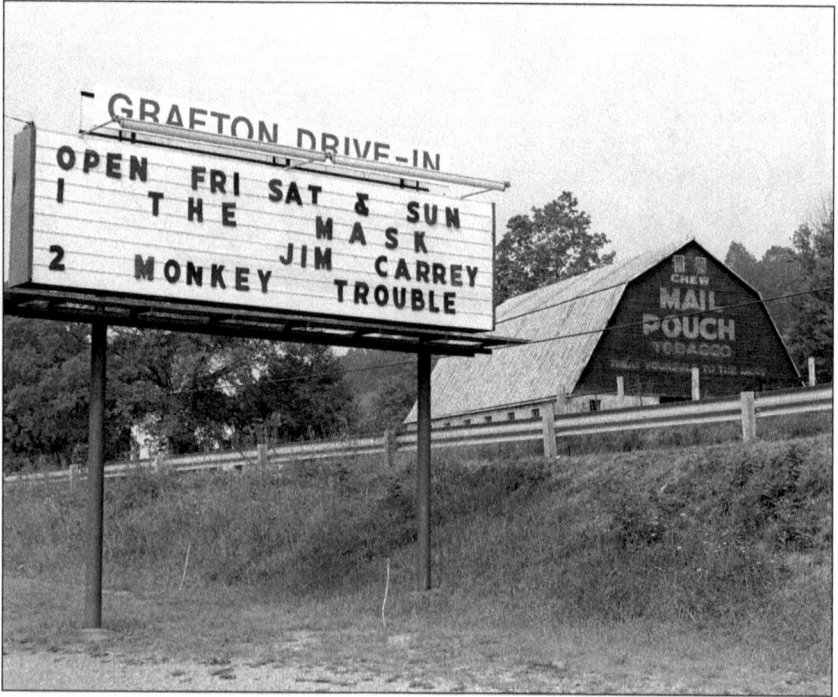

Two once-common sights along the by-ways of West Virginia were captured in this image from 1994: a drive-in theater sign and Mail Pouch barn. The barn was part of the cattle farm that pastured livestock around the Grafton's screen.

"Last week I had one who was sleeping up a storm," John Shingleton said. "I thought I'd have to break the glass to get him to wake up."

Shingleton's job also involved keeping an eye out for patrons attempting to bypass the ticket booth. If a lone driver popped open the car trunk immediately upon parking, there was a good possibility he was unloading more than a cooler. And if someone was caught sneaking into the theater through the exit side, a fine of $50 was levied.

The drive-in theater owner's biggest worry was weather, not freeloaders. And in the mountains, weather could destroy one night's revenue or an entire lifetime of work in a few seconds.

"We had a storm, tornado, come through here in April 1991 and demolish the right side of the screen," Mary Ruth recalled. "We had planned on opening up that weekend and had to postpone it until we could rebuild the screen. I know of at least two other times it was blown down."

"Windstorms have blown it down a good many times," Junior said. "This valley brings the wind right up through it."

Fog was another issue for the low-lying drive-in. Fog passes were issued if the blanket rolled in during the first film. "We are at the mercy of the elements," Junior observed.

Being outdoors also presented challenges from the native population.

"We've had deer run right across the screen," Junior said. "We've counted as many as 20 to 30 deer up behind the screen . . . we have birds fly through the beam, especially in the early evening when they are going after the bugs."

But when the weather, aging projectors, and Hollywood cooperated, an evening at The Grafton Drive-In was a nostalgic journey for the pre-Woodstock crowd, an exciting new experience for the video generation.

"I think it's a great thing," Jim Henderson said. "If you don't go to a drive-in, you're missing something. I think people who do not go to a drive-in are missing a great opportunity . . . I look at the drive-in as something like an amusement park, because you got all that grass."

Jim told me that 1994 had been a good year for both The Grafton and Sunset. Both theaters were packed for several films. Over the Fourth of July weekend, the movie and a fireworks display packed The Sunset and it created a two-mile-long line of cars that had to be turned away from the gate

"Business is better than ever. This is the best I've ever seen it," Jim said.

"Drive-ins are coming back full force," said Mary, who was still dabbling in the business by working the Sunset's concession stand. "The thing is it used to be that picture companies wouldn't sell the newer products to the drive-ins. But Grafton can play the new products with the other theaters."

The Grafton survived for another 20 years after my visit, but the expense of converting to digital projection doomed it and many other drive-ins. The Grafton closed in 2014. Some of the infrastructure is still visible and the driveway that led to the theater off the highway is still known as Drive-In Drive.

Mary Ruth Henderson died September 28, 2021, at the age of 78. She and Jim had been married 57 years. Junior Armstrong, a Vietnam veteran and the projectionist, died May 4, 2007, at the age of 65. He is buried in the West Virginia National Cemetery at Pruntytown.

The Warner's Drive-In in Franklin has a mammoth screen and beautiful setting.

Saving Warner's

On the opposite side of the state, at Franklin in Pendleton County, Warner's Drive-In might have suffered the same fate as The Grafton were it not for a grateful, generous community.

The drive-in, located on U.S. Route 220 near Franklin, opened in April 1952. The owners were Charlie Warner and his son, Harold, who built the thing to last. The screen, which has winged walls on each side, is of concrete block construction and has a foundation that could double as a bunker. Standing about 50 feet tall, it is one of the tallest man-made structures in this part of the country.

I visited the theater in 2011, when Jim Hess and his wife, Nancy, were leasing it from Franklin Oil. It was their eighth year of operating the business, although Jim's relationship with Warner's went back to weekend evenings as a child in the audience. Later, he worked at the theater as a projectionist, a job Jim was still performing that night I visited.

While the theater was using an FM radio frequency on which to broadcast the movie's soundtrack, visuals were still coming from a pair of Simplex 35mm projectors installed back in the 1950s. Jim liked the old projectors.

Youngsters chow down on concessions prior to the movie at the Franklin Drive-In on a summer evening in 2011.

He knew them inside out, they were reliable, and the owners had no interest in updating them. But Hollywood did. With the forced conversion to digital projection, Warner's Drive-In closed in 2014 and faced extinction without the upgrade.

A citizen-led effort sparked by a letter to the editor in a local newspaper and social media posts resulted in an effort that raised $60,000 for the digital conversion. A nonprofit group, the Historic Warner Drive-In & Culture Resources Center, was formed to oversee the fundraising and ongoing operation of the entertainment resource.

After several years of standing in the dark, that impressive concrete screen was illuminated again on September 9, 2016. *Finding Dory* played to a packed crowd that night.

Warner's has a capacity for at least 250 vehicles, but because the familiar speaker poles that served to align and space vehicles were removed, capacity is driven by drivers' willingness to "park right." With its location on the side of a hill, all of the spots offer an excellent view. Visit the drive-in's web page, warnersdriveinwv.org, or Facebook page for times, dates, and titles of upcoming movies.

Along the Way: Star Theater

Jeanne Mozier loved welcoming patrons to her Star Theater in Berkeley Springs and serving popcorn from the vintage machine in the concession room, once home to a telephone switchboard.

Single-screen movie houses have become as rare as drive-in theaters, but the Star in Berkeley Springs proves that such ventures can still be viable.

Located at 49 North Washington Street, the theatre helped drive a revival of the entire community's downtown during its ownership by community champions Jeanne Mozier and Jack Soronen.

Jeanne and her husband were "West Virginians by choice," Washington Beltway professionals who fell in love with Berkeley Springs during a trip through the United States. They eventually bought a farm near the community and, in 1977, became the third owners of the community's aging movie house.

"Jack always wanted to come back here," Jeanne told me during my visit to the theater in January 2016. "I feel that I was summoned here."

Jeanne and Jack became interested in the theater shortly after moving to the community. The movie house had been closed for a decade and was showing its age in both appearance and technology. The mammoth popcorn machine in the lobby was from 1949, as were the seats. In the projection booth, a pair of 35mm Brenkert projectors still relied upon carbon arcs for their light source.

"Jack and I took one look at the popcorn machine and old carbon-arc projectors and said, 'We need to own this,'" Jeanne recalled.

Owning a movie theater was not a component of either partner's life dream or business plan. But Jack believed the old bijou could drive an economic revival of Berkeley Springs, which was lacking in retail and entertainment options. And being theater owners made philanthropic sense for the couple.

"This has never been a money-making thing," Jeanne told me. "It's a community service thing we just happen to do."

They partnered with Joe Lillard and purchased the theater from the Lynn family, which had loaned its name to the business. They went to work cleaning and repairing, as well as learning all they could about the building, which had gone up in 1916 as a brick car-storage and supply garage for the Johnson brothers. At that time, the Opera House's Palace Theater was Berkeley Springs' movie house. W.H. Young built both the Opera House and the Johnson Brothers' building.

In the mid-1920s, the brothers renovated the brick garage and retrofitted it as a movie theater. They added a front section, part of which became a lobby. On Monday, April 16, 1928, *The Life of Riley* flashed on the screen of the new theater, dubbed The Berkeley. Both shows were packed.

The Berkeley and Palace survived as competing movie houses in the small town (Johnson leased the operations to different owners), even into the Depression. Six different films were fed through the projectors' gates each week, giving audiences variety as well as value; $2 would have purchased tickets to see all six movies, according to Jeanne's research.

Competition between the houses was good for the community; it forced the owners to add new features, host community events, and upgrade technology. The Berkeley was relatively slow in adopting talkies, however; the first sound films were not shown there until 1932. By 1934, the theater had upgraded to the RCA sound system, the plaque for which was displayed in the Star's concessions area.

Jeanne told me that the left side of the theater's front, now the concession stand, had a variety of non-theatrical uses for many years. In 1937, the C&P Telephone's switchboard was moved into the room and remained there for nearly 30 years.

The theater operated under the "Lynn" moniker until Jeanne and Jack purchased it. Limited to space for only a four-letter word on the marquee, Jeanne, an astrologer, chose "Star" for the venture's new name.

"The name was an inspiration," Jeanne wrote. "We were searching for a name that would convey the aura of movies, fantasy, the whole mystique—one we could use as a theme.... Star was it!"

On October 1, 1977, the Star opened in true Hollywood fashion, with live entertainment, television news cover-

Jeanne Mozier and her husband Jack Soronen in the Star, 2016.

age, and a crowd in costume. The first film to play on the renovated theater's screen was *The Sting* with Robert Redford and Paul Newman. Nearly 400 people came out for the show.

Lillard departed from the partnership early into the venture, leaving Jack and Jeanne in full charge of the Star's destiny. Jeanne took on the role of booking films, which were typically in their third or fourth week since initial release. The theater operated on weekends only, except in the summer, and had but one screen, limitations that made it difficult to get films in their first week or two of release. But Jeanne and Jack compensated by providing an affordable ticket price, reasonably priced beverages and popcorn, and a family atmosphere right down to upholstered living room furniture that replaced the typical folding theater seats in select sections.

The couple sold the Star in 2019; Jeanne, whose name had become synonymous with Berkeley Springs, died Thanksgiving week the following year. Their contributions to saving one of West Virginia's few remaining single-screen houses lives on in the Eastern Panhandle, and it is now in the hands of its fifth owners, Paul and Trey Johanson, who restored the 1928 tin ceiling, replaced the crushed red velvet wall coverings, and upgraded the sound system.

Chapter 9

The Old General Store

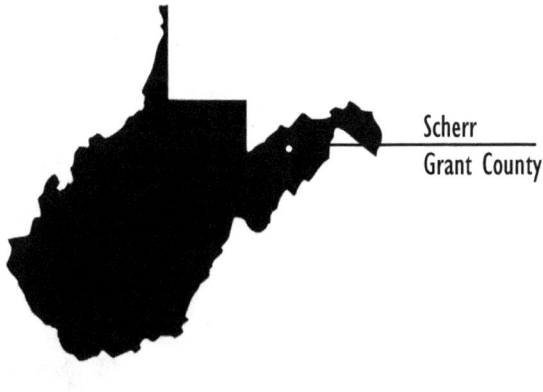

Scherr
Grant County

I went into Grant Kimble's general store at Scherr looking for directions to Greenland Gap, but I got lost in the aura of an old general store.

Grant's store stood at a fork in the road just east of the intersection of routes 42 and 93 at Scherr, an exit off Corridor H. An old, weathered church and the general store define this Grant County crossroads.

A few hundred yards east of this intersection, Greenland Road split in two directions without benefit of signage. Grant said he got his share of tourists stopping for a clarification.

"You want to go to the left," said the soft-spoken, middle-aged man who had been sweeping the floor of his kitchen, a room to the rear of the showroom and separated from it by a cloth curtain. "The sign got tore down not long ago. Somebody run over it," he told me.

Grant went on to say that I would need to take a right a couple of miles down the road, but by that point the surroundings were seriously distracting me. My eyes had adjusted to the dark interior, and they were busily taking inventory of the room. With the exception of the new front door, the Linoleum on the floor, and modern grocery stock, the store

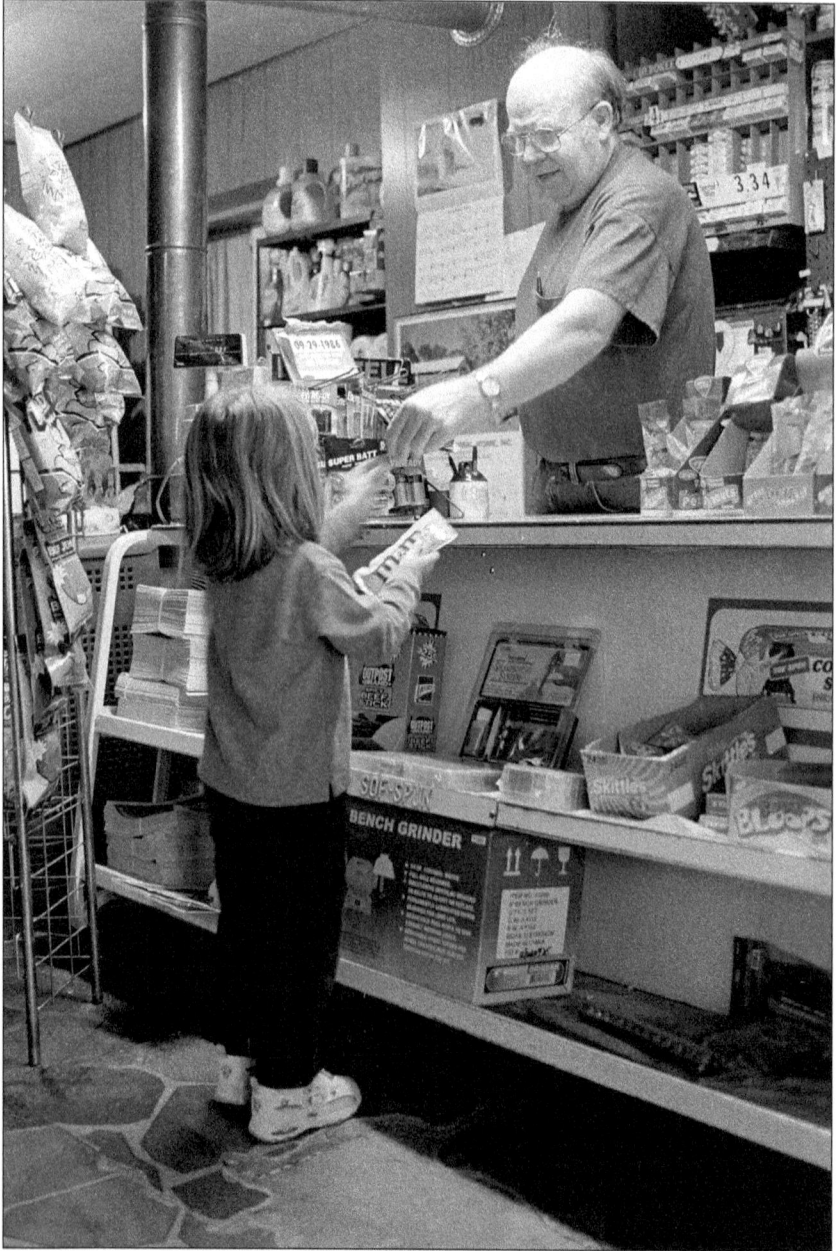

Grant Kimble gives change from a dollar to a young customer at his counter in the former Evans Store at Scherr.

Grant Kimble's general store at 299 Olen Kimble Road, Scherr, September 2004.

looked very much like it would have been seven decades prior to my visit in September 2004.

The ceiling and shelving were made of chestnut lumber. Dating from the era when the blighted trees were being harvested from these forests, the building's skeleton was most likely chestnut, as well.

A circa-1960s US Post Office decal was on the front window; the old wavey glass gave a distorted view of the crossroads. Merchandise was stored and displayed in oak-framed glass cases. A metal Sof-Spun bread rack served as the counter. Behind it was a sales-bill register that held the due bills for credit accounts. The register had been a fixture in the store since the 1930s, when Sly Kimble became a storekeeper. Attached to the top rail of one section of shelves were tickets that stated , "Our ceiling price," artifacts from the Depression-era price controls.

Even the sign on building's roof, "Evans Store," was outdated.

Grant, a reticent, stern-looking, balding man in his middle 50s, told me he'd been working in this store ever since he was 11, when its owner, Jessie Evans and her daughter, Jean, hired him to cut the grass and help maintain the building. Grant got the job because his grandmother and Jessie were sisters.

After Jessie died, Jean ran the store with Grant's assistance. "She worked her whole life here," Grant said of Jean, who died in 2001 at the age of 72.

Grant Kimble at the counter of his store, which carried a variety of goods, the most popular of which were within reach of the shopkeeper.

Jean willed the store to Grant, who'd worked in the woods and farmed while helping the Evans family.

"She told me to do what I saw fit with it," Grant said.

Grant's preference was outdoor work, but age and years of hard, physical labor were catching up with him, and he decided shop-keeping would be a more passive way to earn a living. He worked from 8 a.m. to 9 p.m. every day, except Sundays.

"If I had to do over again, I may not have done it," he said.

One of the issues for Grant was the pressure of competition from the Wal-Mart in nearby Keyser. Grant found that the best way to compete was by keeping the status quo, treating people fairly, and providing services germane to the needs of rural residents.

That included extending credit to established customers. Grant had about 30 such accounts, which ranged from a few dollars to more than $200 in charges for food, boots, gasoline, and anything else the store sold. He expected his customers to settle their accounts monthly.

"It's operated just like it's been done here all the years," he said. "If you

Grant Kimble was postmaster of 26726, which was part of the store for many years. "Everything a regular post office can do, I can do here," he said.

don't do credit business here in the country, you're not going to be here very long because you're too close to Wal-Mart."

Grant also secured and retained customers by providing exceptional service. He'd even pump their gas for them. The store was the community's only gasoline seller, but Grant told me those sales were not very profitable. High taxes levied on the underground storage tanks consumed most of what he made.

Perhaps the most distinguishing characteristic of the store was the post office station based there. Grant had a U.S. Postal System contract that designated his location as a Keyser Post Office rural station. Once a common, coveted, almost essential arrangement for rural shopkeepers, the post office contract gave Grant's store an edge over his high-volume competitors in way of guaranteed traffic.

The postal section was delineated from the merchandising area by a paneled enclosure with a door and clerk's window. Inside the enclosure, Grant sorted the mail into cubicles for the 30 or so box patrons who picked up their mail at the store and the nearly 100 rural-delivery customers

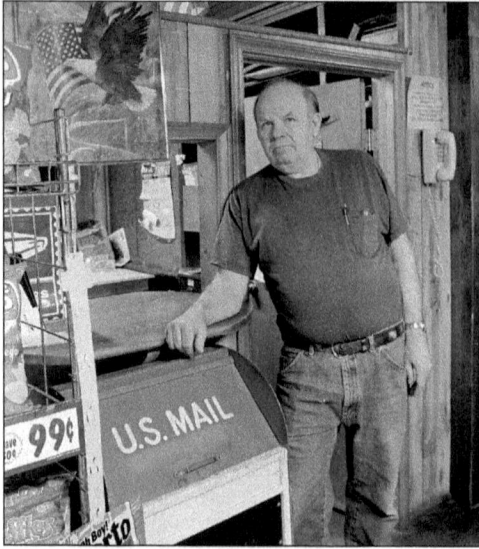

Grant Kimble in his combination general store, gas station, and post office, September 2004. The building still stands, but there was a closed sign in the window as of October 2023.

serviced by a mail carrier. Every piece of outgoing mail was postmarked "SCHERR, WV 26726."

Mail arrived from the Keyser Post Office around 2 p.m. each day. Grant said having the post office in his store ensured that, on most days, a couple dozen people would stop, get their mail, and perhaps purchase something.

The only thing missing from this slice of Americana was the checkerboard and two old-timers dressed in red flannel shirts and overalls hunched over the board. The more likely customer in 2004 was a young mother driving an SUV and stopping long enough to mail a stack of fund-raising requests. The décor was willing, but the lifestyles had changed since the checkerboard era, even in 26726.

"Most of the old people that did that kind of stuff have passed away and the younger generation has other things to do," Grant said.

Before I left the store, Grant retrieved from a refrigerator in the back a recycled iced-tea bottle filled to the brim with a light, golden liquid. He offered it to me and, with a wink, said it was a "little something they make around here." I thanked him, took it home, and put the bottle at the back of our refrigerator. I was certain it was moonshine.

Weeks, months, several years passed. One day, most likely a particularly bad one at work, I decided it was time to open the gift.

The mysterious "little something" was maple syrup.

Chapter 10

Saving the Old Music

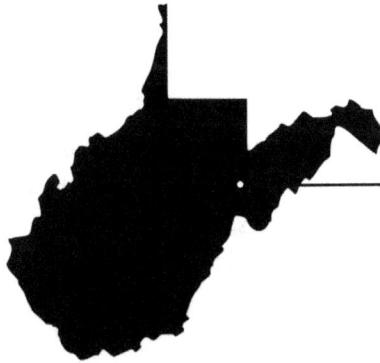

Harman
Randolph County

Ken White often thought about the string bands that played in the Dry Fork region of Randolph County when he was a lad back in the 1940s and 1950s. He thought of fiddlers like Robert E. Lee Kerns, who ran the general store and helped Ken learn to fiddle. With sadness, he also remembered how the strains of their music escaped into the ether without a recorded trace.

"Those old timers, my God, it would have been great if we'd had been able to have recorded them," Ken told me as we sat on the patio of his home along the Dry Fork River at Harman back in October 2009.

The Vietnam-era Air Force veteran dedicated his retirement years to ensuring that the work of contemporary string musicians was recorded and shared with the masses. Working under the name "Allegheny Records," Ken recorded hundreds of hours of performances at shows that he and his wife, Wanda, organized throughout the Dry Fork, South Branch, and Seneca valleys. He also produced dozens of albums for musicians who otherwise could not afford the cost of studio and mastering time.

From these recordings, Ken assembled hundreds of albums, themed collections of old-time songs on compact discs that he burned and distributed one at a time. Ken estimated that he had placed some 70,000 of these CDs in the hands of music fans since starting his work in the mid-1990s.

Outlets included gas stations, gift shops, and restaurants in Tucker and Randolph counties. Ken priced the discs at a break-even point. But the vast majority were provided free to nursing homes, random people he met in Wal-Mart parking lots, Canaan Valley time-share owners, and the musicians themselves. Ken said his work was all about restoring West Virginia's music to its rightful owners.

"This music belongs to the people, not a bunch of damn Mafia members," Ken said as he prefaced his discourse on the evils of the music-licensing industry. "They claim they even own 'Greensleeves.'"

This lifelong passion for old-time and bluegrass music came from growing up in the Dry Fork area, which was infused with string music. He was raised by his grandparents, Issac and Mary Louise White, and aunt, Thelma White. While the family was not musical, string-band music was accessible throughout the region. Ken took an interest in it, and when he was 10 years old purchased a fiddle from an old man whose wife was glad to see him sell it—he was driving her crazy with the dissonance of his unpolished fiddling.

Ken learned to play by practicing with Robert E. Kerns. One day, Kerns asked Ken if he'd trade his $2 violin for a dirty, old instrument that Kerns had taken in as payment for a grocery bill. Ken refused.

"It was a Stradivarius," Ken said. The violin was worth $48,000 at the time; more than a million today. "He tried to give me that thing, and I was too dumb to take it," he said.

He also learned to play the banjo, mandolin, and guitar, and performed in his high school's Future Farmers of America string band, which won the state awards in 1956 and 1957. After college, he had a 23-year career in the Air Force, attained the rank of Lieutenant Colonel, and earned a master's in journalism. While in Vietnam, he teamed up with several other string musicians to form the Gunfighters, which played up to 40 four-hour gigs a month for soldiers returning from the bush.

Ken was given less than three months to live when he was first diagnosed with lung cancer in 1986. He refused to give up and sought alternative

Ken White devoted his retirement to making recordings of musicians in the Dry Fork area, then distributing them on CDs to anyone interested in keeping the old-time music alive. He estimated that some 70,000 of these discs were burned and distributed through his efforts. He was photographed along the Dry Fork River in 2009.

treatment for his disease. Ken credited a herbal cancer treatment for keeping his disease at bay for more than two decades.

A divorce came along with the illness. Ken eventually remarried to Wanda Hale, a Texas native and "lark." He described Wanda's voice as equal to or better than the best professional country performers. Initially, they divided their time between Texas and West Virginia, but by the early 1990s, Ken had succumbed to the mountains' summons. "This is home," he said.

Ken competed in many stringed-instrument contests and garnered awards for his talent. He was particularly proud of his work on the long-neck banjo, which has a distinctive sweet sound, and his fiddling, which uses D-A-D-D tuning. He and Wanda had a television show on an Elkins public station and hosted the weekly *Allegheny Show* on WELD-AM out of Fisher (Moorefield). The show was a combination of his commentary and recordings from the many jam sessions and private recording sessions he arranged.

In the tradition of the early song catchers of the Appalachian region, Ken set up impromptu recording studios wherever he could find a quiet spot, often a public library. He would pull in a few backup musicians from his circle of friends to assist with the projects.

"I'd work them to death," Ken said of the long sessions in which he did double duty as engineer and musician. He said they never rehearsed prior to a recording session or show; it was his plan to make the performance as original and spontaneous as possible. This was done in keeping with the advice the late Woody Simmons of Mill Creek: "Make (the music) your own."

Ken recorded to VHS tape, converted the analog recordings to digital files, sweetened them in audio processing software, and burned the CDs. He estimated that he digitized 4,000 tracks, many of them with him and Wanda as either featured or backup musicians.

The CDs were distributed all over the world as they passed from friend to friend, sold at garage sales, and given away by churches. That was the plan all along.

"Our objective was to get this music out," he said. "It's all over the world. Music is like a virus."

All that said, Ken wanted his legacy to be that of a "mountain fiddler," not a song catcher or distributor.

Kenneth O'Neal White died at the age of 73 on April 6, 2013. Wanda Sue White died April 10, 2016.

The CDs they made still show up at garage and estate sales in the region. Look for the "Allegheny Records" imprint.

Chapter 11

The Roadside Vendor

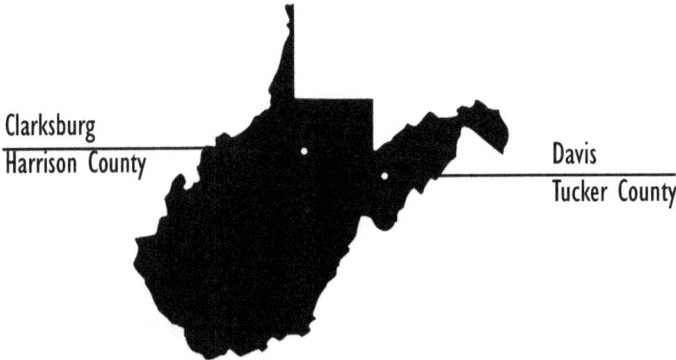

Clarksburg
Harrison County

Davis
Tucker County

Travel West Virginia's byways in warm weather, and you will likely come across a roadside vendor or two wherever there's a wide pull-off with enough room for a van, folding tables, and car or two.

I confess that I'm a sucker for these "pop-up flea markets." Some of these have become so well established that the same vendor shows up week after week. On the outskirts of Davis, where Route 32 intersects with Corridor H, a honey dealer and birdhouse vendor are there most weekends. On the other side of town, just after crossing the Blackwater River on Route 32, another wide spot often hosts a vendor or two.

Every Labor Day weekend, Louie Palmer appeared at this wide spot to peddle his cherry-apple cider, a regional beverage that Louie sold in half-gallon glass jugs lined up on planks spread across sawhorses. Homemade signs placed a few hundred feet of either side of Louie's stand alerted motorists to his cider and Amish jams and jellies.

These signs encouraged motorists to stop and get a free cider sample. I took the bait, turned around, and pulled in behind his silver Dodge pickup.

Louie was sitting in a chair next to the truck's dropped tailgate. His

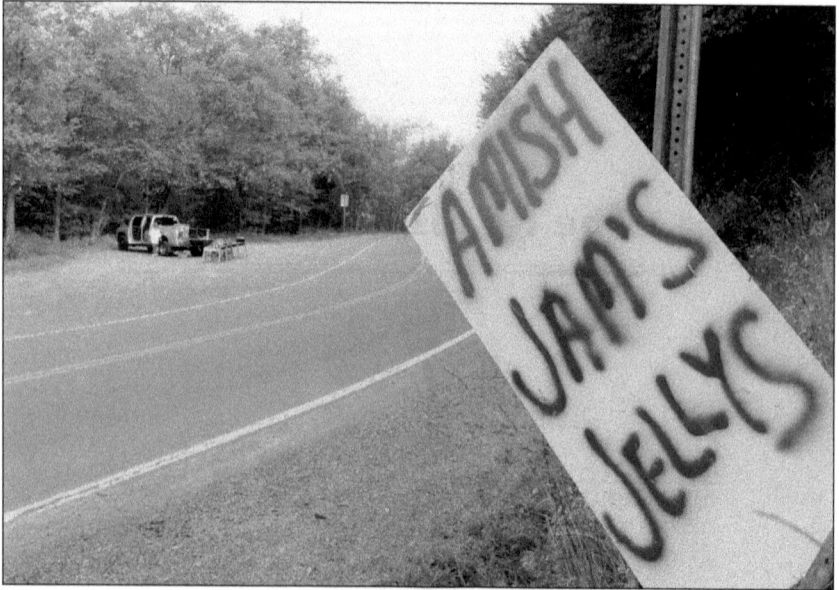

A wide spot outside Davis and along Route 32 and the Blackwater River has been a popular spot with roadside vendors for years. Louie Palmer showed up in the fall.

deeply furrowed forehead was beaded with sweat and was tanned almost to the burgundy color of the cider he was peddling.

He offered me a one-ounce swig from a plastic cup. It tasted like a whole apple and a quart of black cherries were concentrated in that one sip. I handed him a fiver and became the owner of a half-gallon of the liquid orchard. For $9, I could have had a gallon; six half-gallon jugs would have set me back $25. This was back in 2007, when life was more affordable.

Louie's product sold itself. On average, 90 percent of the people who sampled went home with a jug or two. That made Louie's job easy to the point of being monotonous.

"I don't high pressure them," Louie said. "They either want it or don't want it."

Fifty-nine-year-old Louie had been peddling this cider since he was 12 years old. His uncle, William Lee Whitacre of Cross Junction, Virginia, developed the concoction a half century earlier. William grew the apples on his 300-acres Shawnee Canning Company orchard just east of the West Virginia line. The black-heart cherries came from an orchard in western

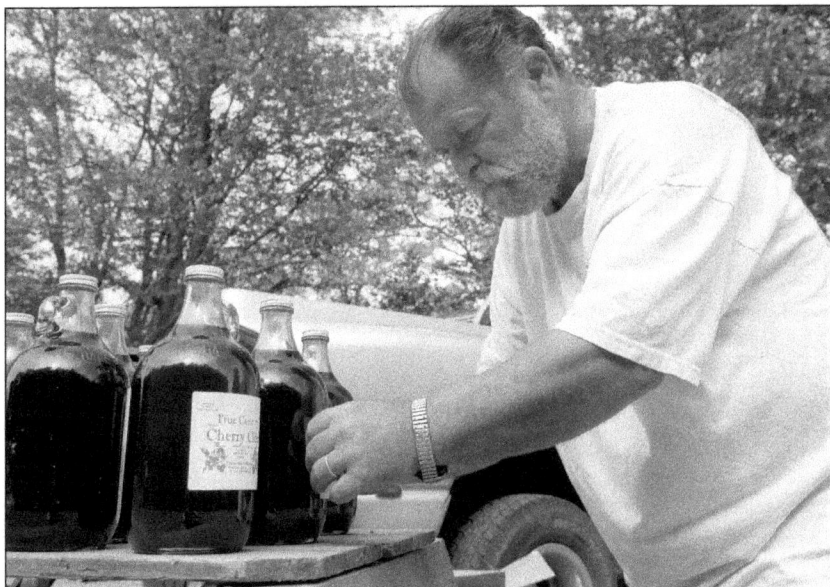

Louie Palmer applies labels to his cherry cider, a regional beverage blended by his uncle, was made from apples and cherries from the tri-state area.

Maryland. The cider was peddled throughout the region and at the family's store in the Winchester, Virginia, area.

Louie had observed his uncle blending the black cherry juice with the cider, made from several varieties of apples, but the exact percentage of each juice was a secret. William sold the blend to Louie, who branded it under his own label and sold it at Davis and Seneca Rocks during September and October.

A resident of Fairchance, Pennsylvania, Louie had been selling in West Virginia for more than a decade when I came across him. He kept his stock at a campground near Seneca Rocks, then hauled the product to Davis in manageable quantities, about 80 cases for a weekend of selling.

He developed a faithful following during his decade at the West Virginia wide spots. Many of the folks bought it as an elixir for arthritis and gout.

"I sold one guy from Parsons four cases (that's 12 gallons). I was sold out of it here by 3 p.m. yesterday and could have sold more if I'd gone back and got it. I would have had a heck of a day here yesterday."

Louie said some customers mixed the juice with Jack Daniels or vodka.

Louie Palmer said sitting by the side of the road could get a little boring at times, but he did not know any other trade, so he kept at it.

"I've heard of them mixing liquor in it and putting cherries in it," he said. "They let it sit in the refrigerator like that. I've heard it's really good, but I've never tried it. I'm no drinker."

Picking up these tidbits from the motorists who stopped to shoot the breeze with Louie helped break the monotony, probably the biggest occupational hazard in his line of work. Some days, like the Sunday that I stopped, there isn't much traffic or many thirsty motorists. Louie broke the monotony by keeping his stand tidy and smoking cigarettes. He took his first puff at age 15, and smoking became as much a part of his job as pouring samples.

"It breaks the monotony," he said, taking a puff from his cigarette.

He also ran Lou's Cider and Jam House on Route 40 in Fairchance. Louie sold the cherry/apple cider at that stand, as well as pumpkins and other local produce. Before she became ill, Louie's wife, helped him in the roadside peddler business.

"I don't know anything else that has ever interested me," he said. "I had a job in a steel mill for two months, but I couldn't take it."

That passion for peddling didn't run in the family, however. His four

A buyer leans in to inspect one of the items on Guy "Mike" Johnson's table full of second-hand merchandise. The author went home with a lamp from the table.

children, Misty, Jody, Louie, and Erik, did their time sitting alongside the road selling cider, produce, jams, and jellies. And each found something else to do as adults.

"I had them all work out here, doing this when they were kids, Saturdays and Sundays," Louie said. "They didn't like it. It taught them to go out and get an education and a job."

Louis "Louie" Walter Palmer died January 31, 2014.

Johnson's Corner

Another roadside vendor location was at the intersection of routes 25 and 98, Clarksburg. The spot, owned by a utilities company, provided plenty of room for Guy "Mike" Johnson's van, five or six card tables, and three or four other vendors.

It was a busy intersection that caught much of the Veteran's Administration Hospital traffic on Route 98. When I visited his corner on a chilly day in November 2003, Mike told me most of his sales were to these

Guy "Mike" Johnson may have been the only man in West Virginia to have had a truck-pull off area at an intersection named for him. His persistent presence at the intersection in Clarksburg gave it the name of "Johnson's Corner." He was at the spot from 7:30 a.m. until noon weekdays.

out-of-town motorists. For the most part, locals didn't want to part with their money or didn't have the dough to part with in the first place.

"People come in here, they ain't got any money, they're on welfare," he said. "I give them the stuff. I had some people come in here, and I gave them a couple boxes of Avon. The kids went from door to door in their neighborhood and sold every bit of it."

Most locals stopped to "shoot the breeze" with Mike, whose pervasive presence at the spot earned it the unofficial name of "Johnson's Corner."

"Everybody knows me," said Mike as he waved at a sheriff's deputy who honked while zooming by. "Even the law buys from me, the city buys off me."

Mike could be found at this spot from 7:30 a.m. until noon or later most every day except Saturdays and Sundays. He reserved the former for going to auctions and the latter for cleaning and testing his purchases.

On this morning in November, Mike's stock included antique kraut cutters, jars of buttons, Christmas decorations, assorted glassware, toy vehicles, three Prince Albert pocket-sized cans, and a gray wine jug that came over from Italy with the grandmother of the woman who gave it to Mike.

Larry Shaughnessy, an antiques dealer who regularly stopped at Johnson's Corner in search of merchandise, dickered with Mike for several

One of the attractions of the roadside market is that folks can come as they are, whether on their way to a picnic or church service. Guy Johnson waits patiently for the next buyer

minutes, then forked over $12 for the jug. That single sale was more money than Mike often made in an entire day of peddling his goods. He said his all-time high for a single day was just $60. "Gentleman" George Snopps, a vendor who Mike broke into the business a couple of years earlier, said he had days when he didn't make a penny.

The stuff that sold, said Mike, were things that evoked memories or a sense of history. "People like to buy a piece of the past," he said. "Something that's gone and ain't ever going to come back."

Although he enjoyed making a sale, Mike did not use the dollar bill to measure his success.

"If you got one friend, you are the richest man in the world," he told me.

By that standard, Mike was a rich man. "If I'm not out here, they will call the house and want to know how I am, what's the matter with me," Mike said. "It's just good people here. I ain't never seen any bad people, just nasty attitudes."

The cup was always half full in Mike's eyes. "We look out there and see a grape; he sees a whole hand full of grapes," said one of the vendors who staked a claim on Johnson's Corner. "We see one car, he sees ten."

His friends looked for him whenever they drove by the corner, even in foul weather. "Johnson sits out here in the winter," said a vendor who didn't want to give his name. "I come by here one day and it was 7 or 8 degrees below zero, and he was sitting out here.

The strange part of that scenario was that people still stopped to look at his stuff.

"I've set up my tables in the snow," Mike said. "People will drive up, get out of their cars, and shiver a little bit, and say, 'Boy, it's cold.' They think I'm kind of stupid to sit out here, but there's no sense in sitting at home. If I sit at home, my legs go bad. I got to keep them moving."

Mike's bad legs were a legacy from a major cancer operation several years earlier. The surgery left Mike in a coma for more than a week and bedridden for several months.

"I died once and came back," he said. "The medicine was hurting me worse than anything else in the world. I couldn't walk. And I said, 'Lord, I can't go this route.' Next thing I knew, I was walking."

Not just walking, but peddling. Although weak, Mike returned to his corner. "I'd come out and (the other vendors) would set my stuff out for me," he said.

Mike's positive outlook, which put him back on his feet after his cancer operation, was dispensed free of charge at Johnson's Corner, along with his wisdom.

"You just can't be thinking negative thoughts in life," he said. "You got to be positive. You got to fix your mind on one idea and stick with it. If you think one way half the time and think another way half the time, you won't get anywhere.

"There's three things in life," he added. "There's nothing for sure, nothing impossible, and nothing forever."

Chapter 12

An Old-Time Auctioneer

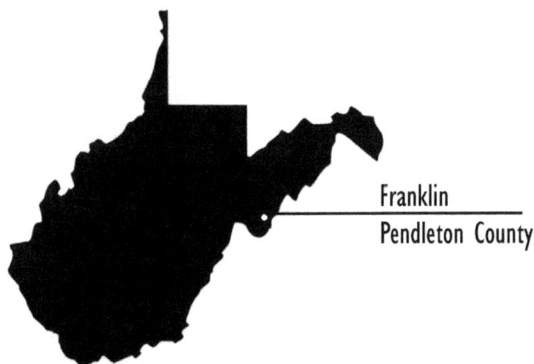

Franklin
Pendleton County

Like those roadside vendors, Garry Propst made his living selling stuff that belonged to other people, most of them deceased. Folks who bought this stuff were often roadside and flea-market vendors or second-hand store owners, which was another one of Garry's ventures

The Pendleton County auctioneer earned a portion of his livelihood from auctioneering for over 30 years. In that time, he sold everything from false teeth to wedding bands. But there's one thing Garry disliked selling to a crowd: guns. And he had a diplomatic way of refusing to sell them.

"I'll say if you're a convicted felon, or if you have ever lusted after any other person's husband or wife, you can't buy a gun," Garry told me back in 2011. "People say, 'Just put them back in the house.' That takes care of it right there."

Garry shared this story while seated at the sales counter of A&P Antiques and Gift Shop, a building next to his home on Route 33 West, a few miles outside of Franklin. Garry was the "P" of A&P and his son-in-law, Bob Alexander was the "A." But when it came to auctioneering, Garry was sole proprietor of the service that he had operated in the South Branch region since the 1980s.

Survival in the business for that many years required being part salesman and part comedian.

"You're an entertainer, you got to keep humor. If you keep people's faces a goin', wearin' a smile, they'll spend more money." Garry said. "If they have a frown, they won't spend it."

Garry had a repertoire of stories that maintained a light-hearted mood at his sales. One of his favorites concerned his personal willingness to get caught up in the excitement of bidding.

"I had an auction where I was selling this sugar bowl, it was a bluebird design. I bought it for my mother and paid way more than what she wanted me to, $255," Garry said. "Afterwards, I heard some kid say, 'Some fool paid $255 for a sugar bowl.' I turned around and said, 'Well, I'm that fool.'"

One thing Garry would not do was slow down an auction's pace with a lot of wisecracks and stories.

"The faster you can go, the more money you can get from it, because folks don't have time to think about how much they are spending. I tell people, 'When you go home broke, I've done what I should have done. I like to send you home with no money and a truck or car full of merchandise,'" Garry said.

Garry was born December 21, 1945, and was raised by his mother, Edith Propst, and paternal grandparents, Charley and Maggie Propst. He grew up about one mile from the center of Franklin, and while he did not have a father in his life, he had many father figures who molded his character and interests. His grandfather was a blacksmith and imparted an interest in old tools and mechanical things. John Harmon was his mentor in business matters. Brooke Boggs, a teacher and farmer who hired Garry to assist him on the farm, took Garry to the livestock auctions and introduced him to the art of auctioneering.

Those auctions were held in Rockingham County, Virginia, where George Heatwole was the auctioneer.

"I used to sit over there and listen to that auctioneer, and whenever I'd get out to where nobody was around, I'd practice a little," Garry said. "That guy over there, I more or less learned his style. He was an old country boy; he was a farmer. I told his son, who is also in the auction business,

Garry Propst points to a bidders in an effort to bring a higher price he lowered the hammer on a sale. Garry was an old-fashioned auctioneer who believed in keeping a quick pace and light atmosphere at his sales. Photo from a 2012 sale at Riverton.

With a wagon full of goods to liquidate in a matter of an hour or so, Garry Propst insisted serious buyers gather around him and the curiosity seekers stay in the background. 2012 auction at Riverton.

'I learned from the best in the business in the state of Virginia; I learned from your daddy, George Heatwole.'"

Garry calls that style the "old fashioned way." "I try to keep it close to the soil, so the average person knows what you are selling," he said of his simple chant, which he compared to the way Bill Monroe kept his music true to its roots.

"We got a True Temper hatchet, here," Garry said, demonstrating his technique. "What is it worth and what will you pay for it? Will you give me a five-dollar bill?"

Allen Pitsenbarger was the dominant auctioneer in Franklin when Garry was an adolescent and young adult. Pitsenbarger also did some farming and lived in a section of Franklin known as "Little Egypt."

"He would say he was an Egyptian, he came all the way from Egypt," Garry said.

It was Allen Pitsenbarger who gave Garry his break into the business.

"I had sold some things at the fire company's annual carnival, and somebody told Pitsenbarger," Garry said. "He was having this big sale in Franklin, and it was getting into the afternoon. Allen was getting up in years, and he was tired. He said, 'Is there anybody in this crowd who could sell some stuff?' His niece's husband motioned to me. I went up there, and, of course, I was scared to death, but I survived."

Garry and Pitsenbarger took turns selling throughout the afternoon. Garry said he overheard a woman say, "Oh my God, not him again," when Garry made his way back to the block after a break.

He was about 30 years old when he began working with Pitsenbarger as an apprentice and without the proper permit. When it came time to get his license, Garry simply had to obtain the signatures of three other auctioneers willing to vouch for his character and abilities. He never went to auctioneering school. Rather, he learned his craft from working with Pitsenbarger, listening to other auctioneers, asking questions, and making mistakes.

When Pitsenbarger became ill in the late 1980s, Garry gradually took over the business and, after the death of his mentor, soon became Pendleton's County busiest auctioneer.

He was licensed in West Virginia and Virginia and conducted auctions as far west as Preston County. His franchise was in Pendleton County, and Garry estimated that he commanded about 95 percent of its auction business.

He built the business through word of mouth and repeat customers. "I always went by the philosophy that every time I had a sale, the man I was having the sale for was advertising for me because my name was at the bottom of the listing in the newspaper," Garry said.

In all his years of doing auctions, only once did Garry have to advertise his business in the newspaper.

"Someone started the rumor around that I didn't do auctions any longer," he said. "I finally had to put an ad in the newspaper that it was just a rumor that I had stopped doing sales, and if you wanted one, just give me a call."

He called his business "Garry Propst Auctioneer." Because there was at least one other Gary Propst in the county, he differentiated himself by adding a second "r" to his first name.

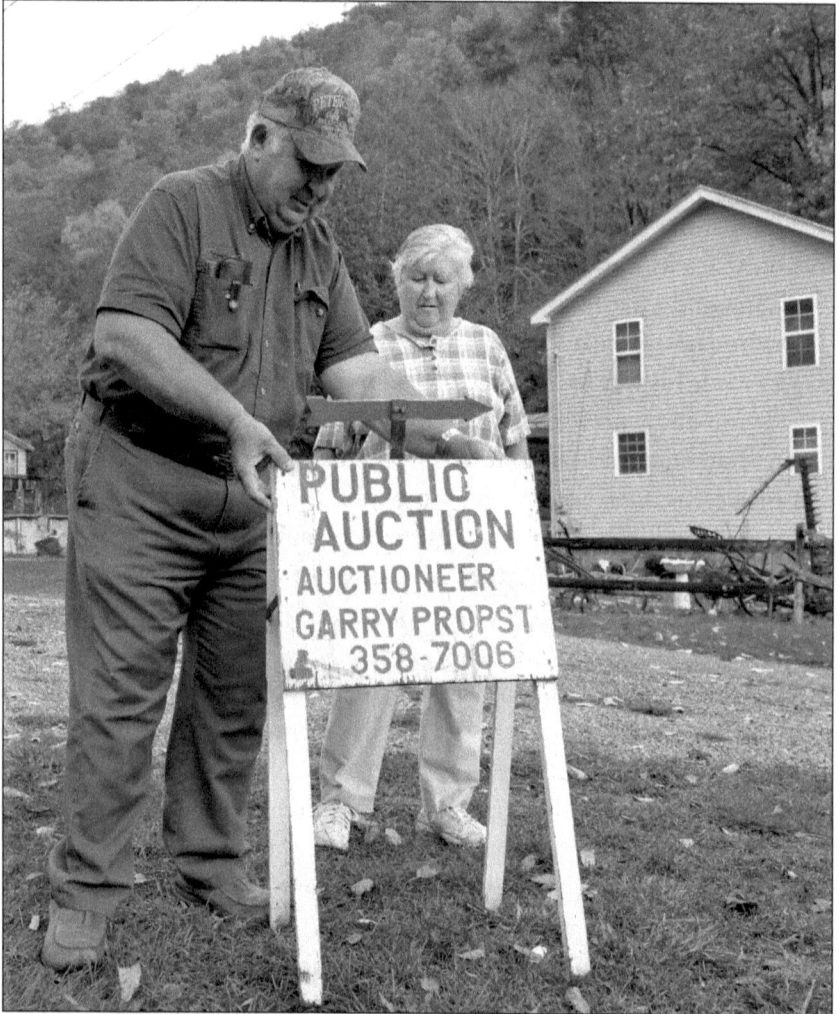

Garry Propst and his wife, Naomi, worked together in both the auction business and their second-hand store in Franklin.

Auctioneering was never a full-time business for Garry, who worked 39 years at the Walker (auto exhaust) factory in Harrisonburg, Virginia. "It's a sideline, kind of hobby," he said.

In his heyday, Garry ran an auction almost every Saturday. He seldom had to use a microphone and PA system because he was "pretty loud" on his own. To further ensure that the crowd could hear him, he insisted that serious buyers separate themselves from those who were there to socialize.

"I'd tell them, 'If you are here to buy stuff, get up here where you can see. If you come here to talk, get back by the fence, where you can talk and have a good old time,'" Garry said.

Garry used cherry-flavored cough drops and grapes to sooth his over-worked vocal cords.

"One thing I've found that works awfully good is to take seedless grapes and put them in the freezer in Styrofoam cups. When your throat gets kind of hoarse, you can suck on those, and you don't even know they are frozen," he declared.

He charged a commission of 10 percent plus expenses. Garry said some Virginia auctioneers were pulling down 30 percent, but he held the line on his fees to give sellers a good return on their goods. At one time, Garry followed Pitsenbarger's business model and charged by the hour. His top rate was $90 an hour, but people balked at that price and Garry was losing business to commission sellers. He went back to the percentage model, but said if most sellers did the math, they'd see that paying by the hour is generally a better deal for them.

Garry typically worked as sole auctioneer at his sales, with his wife holding up items and helpers running the sold merchandise to buyers. He did a few estate sales that required two days to liquidate, and Garry did all the selling.

"I never quit . . . I keep her moving from start to finish," he said. "I had one sale I done by myself and went from 8 a.m. to dark, both days."

He held auctions in all kinds of weather. Garry got a call from a person who wanted to book a sale for the Saturday before Christmas.

"I said that would be the worst day of the year, everybody's got Santa on their minds, and they will all be in Harrisonburg shopping," Garry said. The seller decided the Saturday after New Year's was a better option, although Garry tried to discourage him because the venue dictated an outdoor event.

"When I left that morning, it was 15 degrees," he said. "When I got to the sale, to my amazement, there were 70 smiling faces waiting for their numbers. We had about 170 people out that day, one of my best sales ever. We had primarily tools, and some guns."

Garry Propst relaxes with his dog in the second-hand store that he and his wife operated. October 2011.

Farm sales were his favorite because of his personal propensity for old tools. But he also enjoyed selling dishes at estate sales.

"Pitsenbarger didn't like to sell dishes, so he gave them to me to sell," Garry said. "It seems like I was always able to get a good price for them. We had a sale one day and we were getting ridiculous prices for dishes. (Pitsenbarger) said, 'I know I should go in there and let him rest, but with the prices he's getting, I'm going to just let him go.' I always did have good luck getting a good price."

Debbie Cayton, a cousin, worked as his clerk and had the responsibility of recording the item, the price it brought, and the buyer's number in a matter of seconds.

"(Debbie) was just about mistake free," he said.

Garry said the clerking job was demanding because he relied upon them to remember the details of the sale. His focus was always on the next item.

"Say I'd sell something for $20 to number five, don't ask me 30 seconds later what it sold for, because I have erased that from my mind," he said.

A few years back, Garry was called to do a farm sale and, as was his practice, he walked through the estate to get a feel for what he'd be selling.

"I went up to write up the sale, and they had a couple of pie safes for sale," he said. "I said, 'Boy, we'd be in business if you had an eagle tin pie safe because they are very rare.'

"They had a bunch of stuff in a garage building, and when I raised that door, I was about like Fred Sanford, I'd just about hit the big one. Here was this nice walnut, eagle tin, pie safe looking me right in the eye. I said, 'You can mark down $10,000 for it.' But they all said, 'That old codger is on some kind of drugs, he doesn't know what he's talking about.'"

The day of the auction, it appeared as if the naysayers were going to have the last laugh when the bidding stalled at $4,200. "And then I said, 'Let's get serious,'" Garry said. "And that thing ended up bringing $10,200. That's the highest single item I ever sold."

While listing an auction, Garry took note of a crock marked "J.D. Heatwole," a Rockingham County, Virginia, pottery maker from the mid-19th century.

"One guy told me it would bring about $400," Garry said. "The day before the sale, we had an antiques dealer who was willing to give $900. The man who was having the sale told me, 'You're the boss.'"

Garry said it wasn't legal to sell the item since it was already advertised. The next morning, Garry was hearing rumors of buyers willing to go $1,500 for the tall crock.

"When the dust had settled, it brought $4,000," Garry said. A collector from Virginia purchased it, and Garry learned afterwards that the collector was prepared to pay twice that amount to ensure it would be part of his pottery collection.

Garry's work proved to him that one man's trash is indeed another man's treasure. During the listing phase, Garry noticed that sellers had tossed an old, painted pine board in the trash. It was a handmade sign that read "cabins for rent." Garry's wife Naomi pulled the sign from the trash and put it on the wagon to sell.

"That piece of scrap wood that she dug out of the trash brought $100," Garry said.

Sometimes the intrinsic value of an item drove the price far beyond its market value. When two or more family members were determined to own an heirloom, there was no telling where the bidding would go. Garry

Garry and Naomi Propst outside their second-hand store near Franklin, 2011.

had one such auction where a butter churn went for $1,500. And a corn planter sold for $1,050.

"I tell some people (those prices), and they think I am telling them a lie," Garry said. "But I have the paperwork from every sale that I've ever done, I never throw any of it away."

Sometimes, the person who paid a premium price for an item was the auctioneer. Garry told his buyers that he would bid on items of interest to him, particularly antique hatchets. Over the years, he amassed a collection of some 500 hatchets, many of which were lost in a fire that roared through his workshop in early 2011. Garry rebuilt the workshop, where he and his son-in-law restored antiques, particularly tools and primitive items, for resale at shows.

"It's a headache, something to keep your mind occupied," Garry said, summing up his auctioneering and antiques store. "I'm not going to advertise (for auctions), but if somebody calls me, I'll go."

Auctioneer Garry Charles Propst died March 24, 2022, at his home. He was 76 and had been in the auction business 39 of those years.

Naomi died March 11, 2013.

Chapter 13

The Old Eyesore

St. Marys
Pleasants County

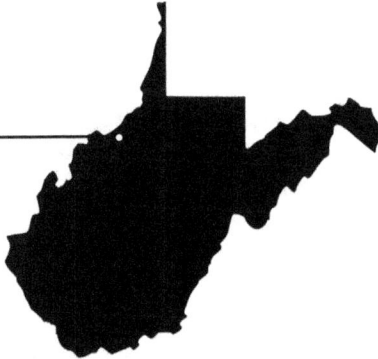

If you have a penchant for auctions, you know that there is a group of buyers who show up for virtually every sale and leave with a van or pickup full of goods. As you watched their overloaded vehicles drive away, you probably wondered, "What in the world is he going to do with all that junk?"

Chester Bills was one of those guys, and he had the eyesore that answered that question. A big sign along Route 2 in St. Marys declared "Bills Antiques and Collectibles," but a smaller sign on the front porch identified his second-hand shop as "EYESORE NO. 2." And Chester and his wife, Betty, were proud of the dubious honor.

The local press bestowed it upon their business following an investigation into sights that would leave visitors with a negative impression of St. Marys. A delegation of Ohio citizens from across the river toured the town and reported their findings, which were published in the newspaper. Evidently, the sensitive eyes of this small-town envoy were offended by all the rusty, weathered, and trampled goods that spilled off the porch and onto the lawn of Chester Bills' Antiques and Collectibles. Being one of the first places visitors encountered upon entering the town didn't help.

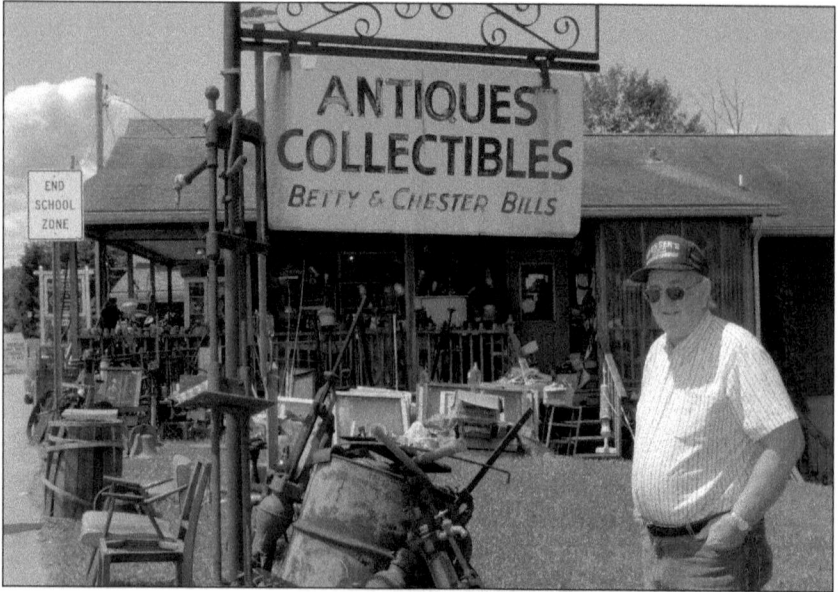

Chester Bills did a great deal of his merchandising along the busy Route 2 highway in St. Marys. His assortment of used goods, mostly stuff he bought at auctions, earned the shop an "eyesore" designation by a delegate of community examiners.

Betty fired off a letter to the editor expressing her displeasure at being named Eyesore No. 2—or being named at all, for that matter. She also had the wooden sign made for their front porch for those folks who were more fascinated than offended by the display of nostalgia-inducing merchandise that beckoned them from the highway.

"There are towns I know that wouldn't put up with it," Chester told me during my visit to his store in 2007. "But (St. Marys) has not done anything about it."

Inside Bills' Antiques and Collectibles, tables and shelves overflowed with the merchandise that Chester and Betty had spent years acquiring at auctions. Like their merchandising approach on the front yard and porch, all items were haphazardly displayed.

"That's one thing I don't do a very good job at, organization," Chester admitted. "I usually wait until I sell something out, then I put something else in its spot. I may not know where the individual piece is, but I know where to look."

Chester Bills said more stuff was stolen from inside the store than from outside, but the stuff outside was more likely to be the victim of an unchecked vehicle or aircraft.

To the best of their recollections, Chester and Betty began selling collectibles at this location, 911 Second Street, in the early 1980s. Acquiring stock came easy for Chester, who was nearing retirement from the construction industry when he went into business. Born in 1927, Chester had been going to auctions since he was 12.

"I went with one of the neighbors," he said, recalling the first auction he ever went to. "I bought a watch, a pocket watch. I gave $8 for it . . . I've been going to auctions ever since."

He specialized in antique engines used in the oil and gas fields around the Ohio River. Chester learned how to restore them and spent his free time hobnobbing with other antique-engine collectors. At one time, he owned over 60 engines. "I liked to hear them run and go to the shows," he said, explaining their appeal.

The best money Chester ever spent at an auction was the dollar he paid for a washing machine with a gasoline engine.

Chester Bills inside his store and next to the monstrous cash register that came from a store in Charleston. Among his unusual items were a viola and golf ball collection. The place was a browser's paradise.

"(The engine) was a rarity, but it was lying in a pile of junk when I bought it," he said. Restored, the engine eventually brought him $800 at a show.

The problem with going to these auctions was that Chester went home with a great deal more than engines. It was with this accumulation that he and Betty, with help from a daughter, Pat, started the store in what had been a rental home.

"I started this shop as a rental property, but (after) I had it rented three months and didn't get any rent out of it, I told the renters I was going to open a shop. I got out of the real estate business real quick," he said.

Just a few months into the antiques and collectibles business, an airplane struck the business location.

"An airplane lost its power and was trying to make it to the (river) bottoms when it hit my mother's house (next door) with his landing gear. Then he hit the roof and chimney (of the store), turned a flip flop, and landed by the tree," Chester recalled.

Betty witnessed the whole thing from her car. The store was closed, but she was at the intersection on the way to work when it came down. The pilot survived, but the building was a loss. They demolished the old house and started over with a new structure.

It was not happy ever after, however. On at least three occasions, brakes failed on trucks descending the Route 16 hill to Route 2. The only place they could go was through side yard and merchandise of Bills' Antiques and Collectibles.

"One came through and got stopped just before he hit the house," Chester recalled.

Despite the susceptibility of his outdoor merchandise, Chester never lost sleep over weather, runaway trucks, and after-hours shoppers seriously impacting inventory. "I get a little bit of stuff stolen once in a while, but not very often," he said. "I've had more stuff stolen from inside than outside."

Two aspects of the business bothered Chester: buyers who balked at paying sales tax and shoppers who assumed prices were negotiable because the merchandise was second hand.

"I feel the public does the antique dealer a disservice when they haggle," he said.

Chester Bills specialized in glassware, but the eclectic stock also included a monstrous antique cash register from a Charleston store, violins and a viola, a golf ball collection, antique toys and trains, old tools, and table after table of household miscellaneous. The stock was but a sampling of the treasures Chester purchased at auctions over the years and stored until the right time. He had at least four buildings and garages "full of stuff."

"I could sell stuff from now until I die, and I wouldn't have to get any more," he said. Chester continued to go to auctions; they gave him a reason to "get up and move around in the morning."

Progress and civic pride eventually prevailed over quirky retailing, and Bills Antiques and Collectibles, Eyesore No. 2, is but a memory on aging retinas. Chester died at the age of 85 on March 24, 2012. Betty died April 24, 2021, at the age of 91.

I immediately took a likely to Greg "Duffy" Ehrhart after he told me the story of "Whisperin' Gracie," namesake of his Route 33 property.

Chapter 14

Whisperin' Gracie

North Fork Mountain
Pendleton County

When it came to business locations, Greg "Duffy" Ehrhart's could have been better.

His Duffy's Mountain Man Antiques was located on a sharp curve on Route 33, about halfway down the west side of North Fork Mountain in Pendleton County.

If you were descending the mountain and failed to navigate the curve, you'd end up in Duffy's driveway, assuming your brakes were operational. Otherwise, you'd likely wipe out the carved Indian at the end of the driveway, crash into the antiques shop, or keep going until you reached eternity. Going up the mountain, you were likely to miss the sign altogether, unless you caught a glimpse of it in the rear-view mirror.

Yes, there were better locations for an antiques shop, but this curve was perfect for a mountain man like Duffy, who adopted his nickname from a mule that he rode to the bottom of the Grand Canyon when he was a kid.

"I'm like a stubborn old mule and an old goat," Duffy told me on a beautiful autumn afternoon in 2014.

Duffy called this place—a rare three-acre clearing between the road and

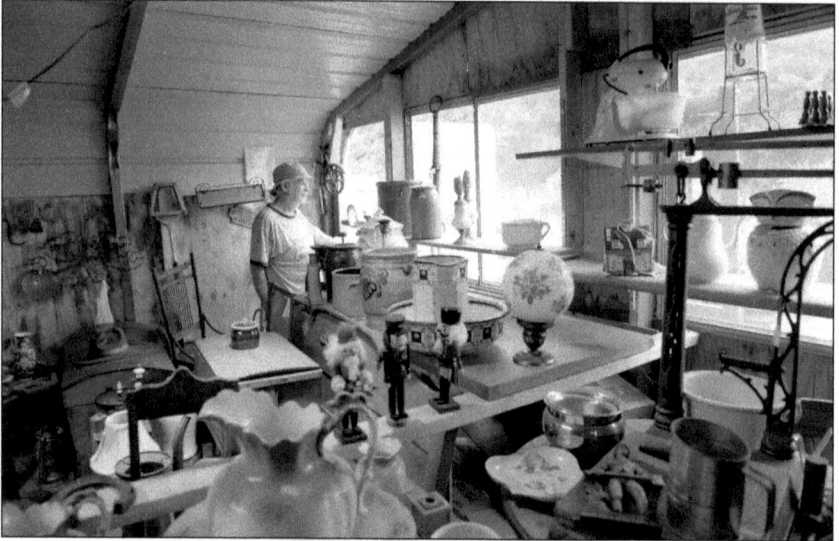

Greg "Duffy" Ehrhart in his store full of odds and ends. His location wasn't the best for retailing, but the view out the back was amazing.

the precipice—'Whisperin' Gracie." I made the mistake of asking Duffy how he came up with that name.

"That's a dog I had back when I lived up in Pennsylvania 10 years ago," Duffy said of the lab/German shepherd mix. "And I'm not talking about her, because I'll cry."

Duffy was a tall, slender guy in his early 60s. He hobbled around on a cane and called himself an "antiques dealer and cripple." His disability came on in an instant and changed his life forever.

"One day I picked up a root ball with a tree on it, and it was all over for me," Duffy said. Prior to the injury, Duffy played tennis 15 to 20 hours a week and worked construction jobs.

"It messed up my back pretty good," said Duffy, who lived in the York, Pennsylvania, area at the time.

Duffy didn't seek Social Security Income for his disability—he wasn't brought up that way. Rather, he did something he'd been hankering to do ever since he was 10 or 11, when he spent a week at an outdoor summer camp. Duffy rented a cabin at a state park, pared back his needs, and lived primitively except for some electrical devices.

Greg "Duffy" Ehrhart referred to himself as an "antiques dealer and cripple." He made the best of the hand life had dealt him after a work-related injury.

He supported himself by buying stuff at auctions and re-selling it at flea markets. "It was great," Duffy said, looking back on those days.

About six years prior to my visit, Duffy and a lady friend decided to tour West Virginia, a place he'd first seen as a child while traveling with his parents. His lady friend spotted the place for sale on the Route 33 curve. "And I thank her for that," Duffy said.

He called the phone number on the sign, met the owner, and committed to purchase the property and its mobile home.

Duffy built a barn for his merchandise and a shed for Molly, his lady's horse. By the time I met him, the lady and her horse were gone, presumably for good.

"She had everything in the shop priced too high," Duffy said. "She went on down the road, and I took all them high-price tags off the stuff. I can't say I missed her, but she took my horse.

"She was the best horse," Duffy said, choking up again. "I wish (the lady) hadn't taken her, but I did buy the horse as a birthday present for her, so I guess she had the right."

Duffy kept a few dogs, cats, kittens, game birds, doves, and "watch-dog goose" for company. The doves resided in a cage on the front porch of his white mobile home with an addition.

"They are here to give me music in the morning," Duffy said.

Ironically, Duffy liked it best when the birds didn't sing, the goose didn't honk, and the tires of careless drivers didn't squeal on this curve. He loved the quiet almost as much as he loved the way storms engulfed the mountain, lightning crackled and exploded in the forest above the road, and the wind banged against his home with such force he expected to wake up on the next ridge.

"It's just amazing to me," Duffy said. "It's about like being 10 feet away from heaven."

Duffy's goal was to make it to retirement age and draw a little Social Security retirement benefit. A veteran, he got his medical care through Veterans Affairs hospitals. His gas and food money came from selling stuff. Duffy admitted it was frugal living and slim eating.

"Since George Bush, things have been bad," Duffy said. "I just want to eat."

His ambition was to become a hermit, to push farther and farther into the wilderness, to gradually fade into the mountain landscape until his Pennsylvania-born dust mixed with West Virginia humus.

"I'm going to stay in West Virginia. They are going to scatter my ashes here," Duffy said, once again choking on his words.

I looked for Duffy's Place the last time I crossed North Mountain on Route 33. The clearing was overgrown and clearly abandoned. That was 2023.

I pray that he's living back in the wilderness somewhere, living on Social Security, and enjoying those storms. And I pray that he's found another dog almost as good as Whisperin' Gracie.

Along the Way: The Old Bus Stop

School-bus student shelter and old car, Route 50 west of Grafton, 2004.

Spend some time driving the back roads of West Virginia, and you'll notice that simple, wooden structures that resemble an outhouse sans door are sited at the entrance to many of the lanes that disappear into up a hollow. Some of these structures have the name of the sponsoring school district stenciled on a side, a reminder of these buildings' purpose to shelter students from inclement weather while waiting for a tax-payer sponsored ride.

In reality, you are more likely to see a row of SUVs and hulking pickup trucks at the end of these lanes rather than students huddled in the shelter. Indeed, I have yet to see one student using a shelter in Preston County, where I live.

One of these structures stands at the end our lane where it intersects with Brandonville Pike. The shelter's roof is rotted and the floor nearly

The Messenger polka-dot shelter, Brandonville Pike, Preston County.

as bad; red oak leaves, not students, gather there in autumn. I have been told by neighbors that it is somewhat of a landmark. Jacqueline Messenger, who lived in the house across the lane from the shelter and was a teacher at Bruceton Mills, painted the structure white and decorated it with polka-dots. Insurance companies, for the purpose of issuing fire protection, reference the lane by this polka-dotted shelter. For three summers, I've intended to re-paint it and replace the roof.

As I wandered the West Virginia back roads, I documented other shelters that were adopted and customized by citizens. Examples of their work appear on the following pages.

Route 219, near the Tucker/Preston counties border, 2003.

Route 16 North, Welch, 2003

This old Preston County shelter still stands on Route 26 north of Valley Point. It was photographed circa 2002, when the drawings were still fresh and legible. I wonder where Heater and Amber are now?

Morris Run Road, Wileyville, 2002.

This one on Route 250 baffles me. Was it for parcels or for short bus riders? The ramp suggests it was intended to be used by the latter. 2003

Chapter 15

Wandering into Difficulties

This beautiful snowfall beckoned me to the back roads and eventually many difficulties in December 2020.

Not all wanderings have happy endings. I have had my share of "wild goose chases" in the decades of searching for stories and at least one back-roads adventure that ended poorly in ways that still reverberate in my life..

The adventure occurred following a beautiful overnight snowfall that transformed the rural landscape into an outdoor studio begging for an outing. I decided to do this one alone, leaving my wife and father at home to pursue their chores while I did a little back-roads wandering on this Saturday morning.

Heading south toward Terra Alta on the pike, I decided to investigate

End of the road: My Scion XD was stuck between a hill and snowbank.

the scenery around a little community with an iconic Methodist church surrounded by farms. Pleased by the images I was capturing from a dirt byway that ran across the ridge overlooking the hamlet, I decided to venture farther along the road, which by now was covered with six inches of snow. No snowplows had touched the lane, but my little Scion XD was handling the fluffy accumulation without a problem.

I traveled the ridge to a cemetery and thought about pulling into its circular drive, but I have this fear of getting hung up in such places. I decided to press on, certain I'd find a plowed driveway in which to turn around.

The road traversed a wind-swept field, then began a steady descent into the forest. The decline soon turned into a deep plunge toward the valley. I had no option but to continue my downward course on a dirt road covered with snow and ice.

"I'll be OK if I keep moving. I'll eventually come to a two-lane road if I just continue moving," I thought.

The road eventually leveled off a bit, but my anticipated intersection with a byway did not materialize. I came to a dead end, a wall of snow that marked the spot where a snowplow had suspended maintenance.

Cinders, shovels, prayers, and cardiac event. The rescue team goes to work on extricating my little back-roads explorer.

I got out of my car and surveyed the situation. In a word, it was difficult. There was a decrepit house near snowbank, but the driveway had not been plowed and the house appeared vacant. I had no cellphone service. I felt like I'd just driven into a nightmare.

Getting my car turned around was not going to happen without a snow shovel. And even if I could get it heading back up the way I came, my subcompact would not climb that steep, mile-long, descent covered in ice and snow. I assessed the options:

♦ Get back in the car, write a note to whoever found me in the spring, then curl up in the backseat and wait for nature to take its course.

♦ Walk several miles to the highway, where I could flag down a motorist in a 4x4 vehicle, explain my predicament, and listen to the laughter as he or she marveled at the stupidity of this old man. I could almost hear the laughter as that motorist shared the story over Christmas dinner.

♦ Walk up the hill until I had cellphone service and call a towing company. But no tow-truck operator in his right mind would attempt taking a wrecker down that hill.

⟋Walk up the hill until I had cellphone service, ask my wife and father to meet me at the intersection, and hope they had a better solution.

The last option seemed the most reasonable under the circumstances, but, gosh, I sure felt stupid. By now, my heart was pounding with anxiety, making the trek up that long descent more difficult. I kept an eye on my phone, and as soon as the "no service" notice turned to one bar, I made the call.

A few minutes later, I met my father in his Jeep at the cemetery and sheepishly explained my predicament. My father, who was 86, agreed that it was best to not risk taking his vehicle down the steep slope. All three of us walked down the hill with snow shovels to the site of my difficulty and embarrassment.

As we examined the situation, I noticed a puff of smoke tinged with the unmistakable scent of burning coal, Appalachian perfume, coming from the chimney of the old farmhouse that appeared vacant. As we worked on digging out a spot in the driveway into which I could back my car, a stooped man with long gray hair exited a side door carrying a bucket full of cinders. He explained that he and wife rented the old house and pretty much depended upon their landlord to get provisions to them during the snowy season. He said there was no exit except to go back the way I came. A bridge that would have given me passage out of there had collapsed years ago, a detail was absent from maps. And, he assured me I was not the first person to end up in front of his house in this predicament, thanks to GPS, which indicated the road was a thoroughfare.

Dad felt that we could clear a path at the base of the hill to expose the gravel underneath and, with the help of cinders, get up the hill to a spot where it leveled off a bit. He could bring his Jeep that far, then use a long rope to start pulling my car up the hill.

We got to work with our shovels while Dad went up the hill to get his vehicle. Meanwhile, the stooped, elderly resident brought bucket after bucket of cinders and wood ashes for us to strategically place along the hill. A sign over his door identified him as a "reverend," but when I asked him about his church, he said it was not a brick-and-mortar kind. He and his wife had moved there from out of state, and they were both renters and caretakers of the property, which included a circa-1900 bank barn.

Consolation prize: Photographing the gentleman who helped us out of the predicament as he went to the barn to feed his feral cats.

The only livestock in the barn were the dozens of feral cats, several of who
followed the reverend wherever he went.

After an hour of spreading ashes, shoveling, and conversation, we were
ready to attempt escape. My father, having grown up with stick-shift trans-
missions, agreed to drive my car and have my wife and I push it. Remember,
that average age of the persons in this trio was around 70.

Between the anxiety, the exertion of pushing, and concern about the
damage done to my car's drive-train, my heart felt like a bullfrog trying to
get out of my chest. I was extremely short of breath, to the point of seeing
stars, but I managed to stay upright and pushing as my father coaxed the
car from cinders to gravel and up the snowy slope inch by inch. After much
spinning, smoking, and sliding, he brought it within rope-length of his
Jeep, which finished the job and delivered my Scion to relatively flat land.

To show our gratitude to the reverend, my father, wife, and I went grocery shopping and filled a couple of boxes with fresh provisions, which we
assumed to be in in short supply at the reverend's home. Dad and I drove

back to the cemetery and put the provisions on a sled that we pulled to the bottom on the hill.

We were surprised to see that his kitchen and pantry were already well stocked with enough food to last a long winter. His wife was seated in front of a television screen about as wide as my car as she surfed the Internet.

I figured his lonely existence at the bottom of this hill would make an interesting Back Roads story for the magazine, and we chatted for an hour or so. He offered to show us the old barn where the feral cats lived, and we followed him and an assortment of cats who assumed this trip signaled an early feeding time. I shot some images of him making the trek, wished him a merry Christmas, went home, and wrote a short entry for my blog at thefeathercottage.com.

A few weeks later, I received a phone call from a woman who said she lived in one of the Western states. She claimed to be a daughter of the reverend and was stunned to see a story about her father on the Internet. She'd been looking for him because there was allegedly a warrant out for his arrest in another state. I won't go into her allegations, but they were disturbing enough that I wanted no part of the drama. I complied with her request to remove the blog post, and she promised to pray for me, something I needed far more than I could have imagined at the time.

A month or so later, that sense of being extremely short of breath that I'd experienced while helping push my car up the hill became so bad I went to the emergency room. My enzyme indicator for a cardiac event was off the chart. Damage from a prior but unrecognized cardiac event, combined with a failing aortic valve, had progressed to congestive heart failure. I had but one option: open-heart surgery, performed a week later.

The surgery to replace the valve and install a bypass was successful, but eight days later, I went into cardiogenic shock, was placed on life support, and transported by helicopter to a Pittsburgh heart-failure unit. The five weeks there were just the beginning of what became a long road to dealing with heart failure that will nip at my heels for the rest of my life.

Like I said at the beginning of this chapter, not all back-roads wanderings have a happy ending! Nevertheless, I continue to wander about these mountains and valleys in my 2013 Scion XD, but not when it snows.

I have become a fair-weather wanderer.

Bibliography

The stories in this work are based upon the author's interviews and interactions with the subjects, often over a period of several days or even years.

Background information for the stories was provided through *The West Virginia Encyclopedia,* edited by Ken Sullivan and produced by The West Virginia Humanities Council. It is available in both print (2006) and online at e-WV, https:www.wvencyclopedia.org.

Readers with an interest in the Priest family of Franklin and the evolution of their mill (pages 90-93) will find a well-researched article by Gary Winkles in the Fall 1985 GOLDENSEAL magazine, pages 18-24.

Dates of passing for individuals featured in the stories were garnered from obituary notices posted by newspapers and funeral homes online, and the author's personal knowledge of the subjects.

Index

About the Author

Carl with Edison, his version of "Whisperin' Gracie."

Carl E. Feather is a seventh-generation Preston County resident; his fourth great-grandparents, Jacob and Mary Feather (Vätter), settled at Crab Orchard in 1803. The story of his German-Swiss Palatinate immigrant ancestors and their relationship to the Allegheny Mountains is told in *My Fathers' Land,* also by Carl. His book, *Mountain People in a Flat Land* (Ohio University Press), relates the story of migration from West Virginia to Ohio in the post-World War II years.

Carl is married to Ruth Evans Feather, a Certified Ophthalmic Technician originally from eastern Pennsylvania. Carl and Ruth have been Bruceton Mills, West Virginia, residents since 2020.

A retired journalist and professional photographer, Carl has freelanced for West Virginia's traditional life magazine, *GOLDENSEAL,* since the mid-1980s, and more than 100 of his stories have been published on its pages. He continues to write and shoot for the quarterly. Follow his adventures and video at his website/blog, thefeathercottage.com.

Wander More W.Va Back Roads

If you enjoyed this book, please consider other titles in this series, as well as *My Fathers' Land,* and Carl's books about another aspect of Appalachia—Ashtabula County, Ohio. All books in this series are available from our online bookstore, Books.by/feather-cottage-media.

To subscribe to *GOLDENSEAL* magazine, visit the West Virginia Department of Arts, Culture & History website: https://wvculture.org/discover/publications/goldenseal/.

Other books in this series:

More Wandering Back-Roads West Virginia
Even More Wandering Back-Roads West Virginia
Still More Wandering Back-Roads West Virginia
Wandering Tucker County, West Virginia (2025)
Wandering Route 50 West Virginia (2026)
(all with Carl E. Feather)

As an independent author and publisher, reviews are our lifeline to gaining new readers.
Please support our work by reviewing this book at
amazon.com
good reads.com.

Booksellers: We would love to have you stock our independently published books. Please send your inquiry to
carl@thefeathercottage.com.

Order Feather Cottage Media books online at

books.by/feather-cottage-media

www.ingramcontent.com/pod-product-compliance
Lightning Source LLC
Chambersburg PA
CBHW052044090426
42739CB00010B/2040